COS TA RICA

T0349365

Travel with Marco Polo Insider Tips

MARCO POLO
TOP HIGHLIGHTS

PARQUE NACIONAL TORTUGUERO ⭐1
Monkeys, crocodiles, turtles – glimpse them all on a boat tour through the canals and lagoons of this fascinating national park on the Caribbean coast.
📷 *Tip: take a series of photos of the crocodiles and combine them using Photoshop.*

➤ p. 96, Caribbean Coast

IRAZÚ VOLCANO ⭐2
From the crater's edge, you can see both the Atlantic and the Pacific at the same time.
📷 *Tip: come early in the morning when the view from the volcano is perfect, at least in the dry season.*

➤ p. 58, Central Plateau

AERIAL TRAM ⭐3
Glide above the rainforest in a cable car (photo).

➤ p. 52, Central Plateau

PARQUE NACIONAL MANUEL ANTONIO ⭐4
Dreamy white beaches and verdant, subtropical plant life form a lush backdrop in this national park near Quepos.
📷 *Tip: stop at the highest point on the access road for a bird's eye view over the park.*

➤ p. 85, Pacific Coast

PARQUE NACIONAL RINCÓN DE LA VIEJA ⭐5
Two volcanoes and over 250 bird species, plus hot springs and a number of different vegetation zones, draw visitors to this national park.

➤ p. 73, The Northwest

RESERVA BOSQUE NUBOSO SANTA ELENA ⭐8

Muddy, slippery and full of adventure: numerous trails lead you through the cloud forest.
📷 *Tip: wait until the sun's rays mix with the mist to create a mystical setting for the jungle plants!*

➤ p. 66, The Northwest

MUSEO DEL ORO PRECOLOMBINO ⭐

San José is home to Costa Rica's greatest treasure: here, all that glitters is indeed gold.

➤ p. 44, Central Plateau

VALLE OROSÍ ⭐

Fabulous landscape, nature, buildings and culture!

➤ p. 60, Central Plateau

TURTLE BEACH ⭐7

The turtles lay their eggs on the beaches of the Tortuguero National Park between July and October – a fascinating nocturnal spectacle.

➤ p. 97, Caribbean Coast

PUERTO VIEJO DE TALAMANCA ⭐10

Experience the real feel of the Caribbean – much more than just reggae.
📷 *Tip: there is a festival in the town almost every weekend – the perfect setting for lively photos.*

➤ p. 99, Caribbean Coast

CONTENTS

38   REGIONAL OVERVIEW

40   CENTRAL PLATEAU
44 San José & around
49 Heredia & around
53 Alajuela & around
56 Cartago & around

62   THE NORTHWEST
66 Monteverde
70 Laguna de Arenal
72 Liberia & around
74 Península de Nicoya

78   PACIFIC COAST
82 Puntarenas & around
84 Quepos & around
85 Uvita & around
88 Península de Osa
90 Golfito & around

92   CARIBBEAN COAST
96 Tortuguero
98 Cahuita
99 Puerto Viejo de Talamanca
& around

CONTENTS

MARCO POLO TOP HIGHLIGHTS
2   Top 10 highlights

BEST OF COSTA RICA
10   ... when it rains
11   ... on a budget
12   ... with children
13   ... classic experiences

GET TO KNOW COSTA RICA
16   Discover Costa Rica
19   At a glance
20   Understand Costa Rica
23   True or false?

EATING, SHOPPING, SPORT
28   Eating & drinking
32   Shopping
34   Sport & activities

MARCO POLO REGIONS

38   Regional overview

DISCOVERY TOURS

104   From San José through
      national parks to the
      Caribbean coast
107   From San José to the Pacific

109   On foot through the
      Curi-Cancha cloud forest

GOOD TO KNOW

112   **HOLIDAY BASICS**
      *Arrival, Getting around,
      Emergencies, Festivals & events,
      Essentials, Weather*

120   **USEFUL PHRASES**
      *There's no need to be lost for
      words*

122   **HOLIDAY VIBES**
      Books, films, music & blogs

124   **TRAVEL PURSUIT**
      The MARCO POLO holiday quiz

126   **INDEX & CREDITS**

128   **DOS & DON'TS**
      *How to avoid slip-ups and
      blunders*

⊙   Plan your visit

$–$$$ Price categories

(*)   Premium-rate phone number

   Eating & drinking

   Shopping

   Nightlife

🌴   Top beaches

(📖 A2) Refers to the removable pull-out map
(📖 a2) Additional map on the pull-out map
(0) Located off the map

The sloth – *Bradypus variegatus* – can be found in Costa Rica's rainforests

BEST OF
COSTA RICA

Perfectly shaped: the Arenal Volcano is recognisable from afar

BEST ☂

WHEN IT RAINS

ACTIVITIES TO BRIGHTEN YOUR DAY

SOLID GOLD!
As you'd expect, the National Bank of Costa Rica in San José has gold bars in its vaults. But it is also home to plentiful gold in the *Museo del Oro Precolombino*, with jewellery from earrings to bracelets and necklaces, plus figures of deities and animals, dating from a dozen centuries ago.
➤ p. 44, Central Plateau

ART NOUVEAU CAFÉ
The *Alma de Café* in the capital's Teatro Nacional radiates the atmosphere of its turn-of-the-20th-century origins. Murals, black-and-white photos, Art Nouveau lamps and marble: it's the perfect place to spend an afternoon.
➤ p. 45, Central Plateau

COFFEE AT THE VOLCANO
The traditional coffee plantation *Doka Estate* (photo), on the slopes of the Poás Volcano, introduces you to the world of roasting and grinding. The buffet at its restaurant is delicious, and there are colourfully painted metal mugs and coffee chocolates for sale in the shop.
➤ p. 55, Central Plateau

SEALIFE, NOT TRAINS
The site of the old railway station at Puntarenas has been turned into the *Parque Marino del Pacífico* – with aquariums, turtle and crocodile terrariums, pelican aviaries and a petting pool.
➤ p. 82, Pacific Coast

THROUGH THE RAINFOREST
Waterproof footwear and a rain jacket: that's all that is required to enjoy the *Parque Nacional Manuel Antonio*. It stays warm during the rainy season, when there are not so many visitors, and a dense leaf canopy offers protection against the downpours.
➤ p. 85, Pacific Coast

BEST ON A BUDGET

FOR SMALLER WALLETS

ART ON MONDAYS

A favourite spot in San José for students and art-lovers: on Mondays, artists display their paintings and installations at the *Museum of Contemporary Art and Design*, a former liqueur distillery with all the industrial charm of an old factory building.
➤ p. 46, Central Plateau

MUSEUM FOR A NATIONAL HERO

In a historic building opposite the central park in Alejuela is the *Museo Histórico Cultural Juan Santamaría*. The Costa Ricans love the building because cultural events are often held here – and admission is free.
➤ p. 54, Central Plateau

"HOUSE OF THE DREAMER" IN THE OROSÍ VALLEY

The outside of *Casa del Soñador*, built from old wood, is inset with lifelike carved wooden figures. On the inside are shelves with numerous works produced by a wood carver and sculptor: a universe of fantasy characters and the country's revered saints.
➤ p. 61, Central Plateau

OPEN-AIR FILMS BY THE WATER

Casablanca, Forrest Gump, Out of Africa: classics and blockbusters are shown at the free *Outdoor Movie Nights* in Quepos between January and March. Make yourself comfortable in the open-air theatre by the harbour, get yourself a beer – and enjoy!
➤ p. 84, Pacific Coast

PALM-FRINGED BEACHES AND A CORAL REEF

Parque Nacional Cahuita on the Caribbean coast is famous for, among other things, its marine flora and fauna. There are two entrances, and access is free (donations gratefully accepted) via Kelly Creek near Cahuita, which is close to wonderful sandy beaches (photo).
➤ p. 99, Caribbean Coast

BEST
WITH CHILDREN

FUN FOR YOUNG & OLD

ADMIRE THE BUTTERFLIES

As big as the hand of a man and unbelievably colourful: at the lovingly designed *Spirogyra Butterfly Garden* in San José, visitors of all ages can discover fabulous butterflies – and learn about them, too.

➤ p. 47, Central Plateau

RAINFOREST AERIAL TRAM

Children of five and older can glide through the rainforest treetops on the *Aerial Tram*, provided they are accompanied by an adult. It's incredible what you can discover up there!

➤ p. 52, Central Plateau

BOSQUE ETERNO DE LOS NIÑOS (CHILDREN'S ETERNAL RAINFOREST)

In 1986, the jungle region of Monteverde gained considerable international fame thanks to the Children's Eternal Rainforest project, for which children worldwide collected donations. The *Bosque Eterno de los Niños* also has a child-friendly visitor centre and great educational trails for little ones.

➤ p. 67, The Northwest

PACIFIC MARINE PARK

Tomorrow's marine biologists will find a crocodile nursery, lots of turtles, sharks, manta rays and tropical fish in the *Parque Marino del Pacífico* in Puntarenas. Expert information is also provided.

➤ p. 82, Pacific Coast

WATCH THE JUNGLE DOCTORS

A baby jaguar that's being bottle fed, or a tiny howler monkey with an injured hand: at the *Centro de Rescate Jaguar* near Puerto Viejo de Talamanca, children can experience how jungle animals are nursed back to strength before being reintroduced to the rainforest (photo).

➤ p. 100, Caribbean Coast

BEST ⚑
CLASSIC EXPERIENCES

ZIP OVER WATERFALLS
Glide effortlessly through the jungle on a zip line. The *Adventure Park* at Hotel Vista Golfo has two dozen different zip lines taking you over 11 waterfalls and various other sights: quite an adventure – even for the less athletic.
➤ p. 37, Sport & Activities

ON THE TRAIL OF THE BLUE-JEANS FROG
Bright blue legs, a red body – the blue-jeans dart frog is the most striking and prettiest of the many types of frog found in Costa Rica. This little fellow is found in most of the national parks, and also in the *Frog Garden* of the *Braulio Carillo National Park*. Spotting one is said to bring you luck!
➤ p. 52, Central Plateau

HIKE AROUND A VOLCANO CRATER
Not only can you climb the *Poás Volcano*, but you can also walk round its crater. A path then takes you through dense vegetation to a second crater with a lake – dress warmly!
➤ p. 55, Central Plateau

BUTTERFLY GARDEN
A creature that is as beautiful as a flower and flies like a bird: admire the wonder of butterflies at the *Butterfly Conservatory* beside Lake Arenal.
➤ p. 71, The Northwest

CAIMANS & MANATEES
The swamps, lagoons and mangrove forests of the huge *Tortuguero National Park* are home to countless animals. What could be more delightful than cruising the waters by boat and spotting exotic birds, manatees and caimans (photo)?
➤ p. 96, Caribbean Coast

GET TO KNOW COSTA RICA

The joy of living: a colourful façade in San José

DISCOVER COSTA RICA

The Playa Espadilla is considered to be one of the most beautiful Pacific beaches

Forests enveloped in morning mist, bubbling volcanoes that light up the night sky with glowing red magma, butterflies the size of your palm and tiny hummingbirds. Trekking through the cloud forest, canoe trips across Caribbean lagoons, a sundowner on a lookout terrace high above the Pacific, or a visit to an organic coffee plantation. These are just some of the sights and experiences you can only have in Costa Rica, and they will leave any all-inclusive luxury beach holiday in the shade.

GREEN, GREENER, COSTA RICA

Costa Rica, a country without war or cold weather and one of America's oldest democracies, is located right at the midpoint between North and South America. It's bordered by two oceans: at the narrowest point, a mere 140km separate the

From 500 BCE
Three indigenous peoples shape the land: the Huetares, Chorotega and Boruca

800–1400 CE
The heyday of Guayabo, a Huetares settlement close to what is now Cartago

1502
Christopher Columbus lands on the island of Uvita off Puerto Limón, and calls the land Costa Rica ("Rich Coast")

1563
The Spanish establish Cartago and make it their capital

1821
Independence from Spain. Costa Rica becomes part of the Mexican Empire

Caribbean coast in the east from the Pacific Ocean in the west. In between, you find mountains and volcanoes over 3,000m. And, probably unique in the world: over one-quarter of this country is protected – as national parks and biosphere reserves, or indigenous reservations and UNESCO World Heritage Sites. Steaming rainforests, mist-shrouded high valleys, ochre savannahs, mangrove swamps and dry forests; mountain chains and volcanoes; meandering rivers, coral reefs and green islands off the coast: they are all part of this country's unusual beauty, and worthy of protection. And, as a bonus, there are many fabulous botanical gardens to explore, which will broaden your knowledge of Costa Rica's amazing flora.

PASSIONATE CONSERVATIONISTS

It's small wonder that Costa Rica has become synonymous with eco-friendly activity holidays, and a place of pilgrimage for ecologists and biologists. In fact, in many respects the country embodies the ideal of the unspoiled tropical paradise. Yet the situation once looked pretty dire – two-thirds of the rainforest had fallen victim to mankind's greed for money before the government realised the danger, listed various areas as protected zones and issued more stringent conservation laws. However, there were other reasons behind these actions: the country's income from coffee and banana exports was not sufficient to cover its foreign debt and balance the state budget. This made it even more vital that the country preserve its most important resource, nature, and make the rainforest

1848
Proclamation of a republic

1948
José María Figueres Ferrer becomes president and a year later the army is disbanded

1987
President Óscar Arias Sánchez receives the Nobel Peace Prize for his service in the Nicaragua conflict

2022
Rodrigo Alberto Chaves Robles, a member of the Partido Progreso Social Democrático, is elected Costa Rica's president

2022/2023
Costa Rica bounces back to pre-pandemic visitor numbers, and exceeded them in 2023

economically viable without destroying it – a difficult task that Costa Rica has aimed to accomplish by marketing the forest to tourists.

The tourist flow that began a number of years ago is indeed bringing in much-needed currency, and today accounts for about one-tenth of the country's employment. Costa Rica has learnt from the mistakes made by other countries: quality instead of quantity is the motto here. Eco-tourism is the order of the day. This includes lower hotel buildings that blend with the landscape and are made from natural materials, and choosing local products over imports.

RECORD-BREAKING BIODIVERSITY

Visitors can follow specially-made *senderos*, hiking trails that meander through the natural parks, for an initial impression of the sheer variety of tropical flora and fauna. The statistics are mind-blowing: 900 tree species; 1,200 orchids; 230 mammal species, including jaguars, pumas, coatis, monkeys, sloths, anteaters and raccoons; 860 bird species, including 53 different hummingbirds and 15 parrots; and 40,000 types of insect, including 3,000 different species of butterfly. This country, which covers around 0.01 per cent of the total surface of the earth, is home to five per cent of all the flora and fauna on the planet: this is extraordinary!

CANDY COLOURS ON THE CARIBBEAN COAST

"Our temples and palaces are our nature," goes the Costa Rican saying – and there are only a few remaining man-made structures dating back to the pre-Columbian period. Before Columbus's arrival, three indigenous tribes lived in what is now Costa Rica, in the shadow of the Mayans who had settled to the north. Instead of palaces, temples and monumental architecture, they left only a few small settlements behind, but they also left ceramics, stone artefacts, carved figures and jewellery. Among these remnants is an assortment of over 300 petrospheres – the mysterious stone spheres of the Boruca people.

Today, the Caribbean love of life is reflected in the wooden houses on the Caribbean coast, painted in bright shades of turquoise, yellow and pink. Some are on stilts, and almost all of them have an all-round veranda.

JOI DE VIVRE IN PARADISE

Visitors love Costa Rica's climate, beaches and jungle, as well as the warm Caribbean vibe and zest for life. Many from abroad have settled here: American Quakers, who cleared the forests to develop dairy farming and agriculture; pensioners, who wanted to enjoy a better standard of living than at home; and even eco-settlers who wanted to live and work in harmony with nature. This doesn't mean the country is without problems. Unsolved issues include high population growth, which is putting additional pressure on residential areas and creating a need for new jobs. Nevertheless, this tiny country manages to embody an exemplary model of eco-friendly living. Discover Costa Rica and you'll discover *pura vida* – pure life!

AT A GLANCE

5.18 million
inhabitants

Denmark: 5.88 million

1,400km
of coastline

Wales: 2,704km

51,100km²
area

Scotland: 80,231km²

HIGHEST MOUNTAIN:
CERRO CHIRRIPÓ
3,819m

Ben Nevis (Scotland): 1,345m

20,000
SPECIES OF SPIDER AND
52
SPECIES OF HUMMINGBIRD
live in Costa Rica

AVERAGE AGE
29 YEARS

United Kingdom: 40 years

"MEDIA NARANJA"

is a loving nickname for one's partner: "the other half of the orange"!

5.30am/6pm

Sunrise and sunset are pretty much at the same time throughout the year (+/– 20 mins).

30 NATIONAL PARKS
and 9 nature reserves

COSTA RICA IS HOME TO 5% OF ALL OF THE EARTH'S ANIMAL AND PLANT SPECIES.

UNDERSTAND COSTA RICA

TICOS & TICAS

The Spanish suffixes "ito" or "ita" are diminutives that are used as a sign of friendliness. Thus *momento* becomes *momentito*, a "little moment". However, the Costa Ricans use "ico" as a diminutive, so they say *momentico*, and they especially like doubling this, for instance to make *hermano* (brother) *hermanitico* (tiny little brother). Because of this habit, other Latin Americans call them *Ticos*, and they are happy to be known as such.

GREEN & BLUE

Green and blue are the colours of the landscape here: the green of the banana trees, and the blue of the plastic bags soaked in insecticide that cover them as they ripen on the trees. Today, bananas are a major economic factor in Costa Rica, and the country is the world's second biggest exporter of the fruit. Cultivation and marketing began at the end of the 19th century, and, along with coffee, bananas became the country's main export. It is interesting to note that bananas are a fruit that can be harvested all year round – an absolute exception among tropical fruits.

WHO LIVES HERE?

Some 80 per cent of the five million *Ticos* are white descendants of the Spanish. Only 15 per cent of the population are *mestizos*, that is, descendants of both whites and indigenous peoples. For comparison, in Mexico the figure is 80 per cent. Just one per cent of the population is black, one per cent Chinese, and 1.5 per cent *indígenas*, the descendants of the original indigenous inhabitants. Around 55,000 of the *indígenas* live in 35 small reserves, and are among the poorest population groups. As the right to political asylum is rooted in Costa Rica's constitution, the tiny country has become a haven for many thousands of refugees from El Salvador and Nicaragua. Population growth is high, and the average number of children per family is five. Almost 90 per cent of the population are Roman Catholics.

MOONLIGHT FLIT

Some enjoy them as an appetiser or soup, others like to wear them as jewellery. Despite numerous conventions on the international trade in endangered species, turtle eggs, meat and shells are still processed and exported in various places around the world. Some species of this animal, which has been on the planet for around 100 million years, face extinction. Costa Rica has decided to protect them, and a number of research stations study, identify, protect and raise them. Thousands of turtles swim onto the country's shores from both of the adjoining oceans, laboriously clambering onto the sand in the moonlight when the tide is in, and digging deep holes for their eggs. Some of them weigh several hundred kilogrammes, and their nocturnal progress is therefore as slow as you would expect. This is something tourists are able to watch, provided they observe a few safety measures – no light and no noise. The eggs spend six to eight weeks hatching in the warm sand (provided no one digs them up first), after which up to 100 tiny turtles scramble up through the layer of sand and instantly head out to sea. Sadly, many of them don't make it, falling victim to man, birds and fish.

JUNGLE SECRETS
Much of the country's incredibly diverse flora and fauna is found in its forests. It is not unusual for many of the thousands of different trees in the Costa Rican rainforest to grow to heights of 40m and more. Life in the jungle is lived on various levels: it's dark, hot and extremely moist on the ground, while life in the treetops is largely unresearched. The most stable but also the most sensitive eco-system in the world, millions of years old, has survived climate changes all the way back to the Ice Age; but today it is at risk caused by man and our influence on the environment. Fifty years ago, Costa Rica's rainforest (in the tropical lowland regions) and cloud forest (at heights above 1,000m) covered over 70 per cent of the land. Now just over 50 per cent of land is forested.

MOUNTAINS & TROPICS
Costa Rica is the third-smallest country on the American mainland. Its topography is largely defined by mountains, and is dominated by 70 volcanoes, both extinct and active. This cordillera runs across the country from the northwest to the southeast, and acts like a meteorological divide. The highest mountain is Chirripó at 3,819m. A vast lowland range follows the

Costa Ricans call themselves *Ticos*

The cloud forests in the national parks are home to tiny aerial acrobats

Atlantic coast, a wet tropical region of swamps, lagoons and rivers. The capital, San José, and the densely populated surrounding area lie in the central high plain at the foot of the Cordillera Central. The country's borders between the Atlantic coast (200km) and the Pacific coast (1,200km) are formed by Nicaragua to the north and Panama to the south.

VOLUNTEERS WANTED!

No other country offers as many opportunities for volunteers as Costa Rica, mainly in the areas of animal protection and conservation. The choices range from monitoring turtle eggs on the Pacific and Caribbean coasts to helping out in the nature reserves, caring for injured wild animals and teaching English to schoolchildren. At the *La Flor* finca (see p. 59) volunteers work in organic farming, botanic gardens, and in the forest or stables, and are also involved in teaching about the environment *(fincalaflor.org/english-1/volunteering)*. The *Wayers* organisation *(wayers.com)* offers a wide range of work experience opportunities, with Spanish lessons and accommodation in hostels or with host families. The national parks also often have interesting vacancies.

NATIONAL PARKS FOR NATURE LOVERS

Costa Rica has more than 30 national parks, and several game and nature reserves, alongside privately owned forests and reservations. The latter are maintained by hotels and guesthouses, haciendas, fincas and lodges, as well as animal and nature conservation organisations. Admission charges, donations and tourist attractions (zip lines, aerial tramways and so on) are partly used for their maintenance. Access to the reservations is along specially laid paths and trails *(senderos)* that you can follow on your own or with a guide. As a general rule, do not try to cut costs in Costa Rica when it comes to guides, because without one you will see and understand far less. They are often highly educated, knowledgeable conservationists and passionate about nature and the interests of the Costa Rican population. Visit *ict.go.cr/en/documents/guias.html*.

NICARAGUANS IN COSTA RICA

Many Costa Ricans believe the number of migrants from Nicaragua, which is estimated at between 500,000 and a million, is too high for the total population of around five million. A lot of them have entered the country illegally and are employed for the banana and coffee harvests or as housemaids, earning between US$250 and US$300 a month. Their living conditions are precarious, and they have no access to the state healthcare system, which is free for *Ticos*. Furthermore, migrants from Central America encounter attitudes ranging from mistrust to open hostility, and they are held responsible for the increase in crime. But without them the country would cease to function, because they do many of the lower-paid jobs. Children they give birth to in Costa Rica are automatically Costa Rican nationals, and so can hope for a better future.

TRUE OR FALSE?

LITTLE SWITZERLAND

Costa Rica is often compared to the Alpine republic. The *Ticos* live a life that many of their neighbours can only dream of. Because the country's breathtaking nature has been protected, tourism brings the country significant revenues and the economy functions well. The small Central American country is also a much-cited exception in terms of its cleanliness. It is hardly surprising that many Swiss citizens have become expats here. And there is another similarity: Costa Rica increasingly attracts high-tech companies, such as chip manufacturer Intel, which runs a regional research centre in the country with further projects planned.

PURA VIDA

You will hear these words a lot in Costa Rica. "Pure living" is far from being a PR gimmick. Instead, it is a philosophy for life, both a greeting and a farewell, a solace in difficult times, and confirmation that life as it currently presents itself is OK. Actually, no, not just OK, but good and right. The *Ticos* know that worrying too much doesn't help – they prefer to live in the moment, and are masters at staying relaxed even when life gets tough.

HEALTH INSTEAD OF ARMS

In 1948, a time of political unrest, rebel group commander and social democrat José Figueres Ferrer became de facto leader of the government for 18 months. He launched effective social reforms and, a year later, submitted a constitution that included the abolition of the armed forces. This measure has paid off for Costa Rica in many different ways. The money saved was invested in social welfare and healthcare, in teaching the population to read and write, and in a comprehensive reform of the education system. Today, Costa Rica is unique in Latin America for these achievements – and has not suffered in any way from the absence of an army.

ECO

Costa Rica is the world's leading destination for eco-tourism. Today, you will be hard put to find a hotel or provider that doesn't have the word "ecological" or "eco" in its name. However, as the popularity of this tiny country grows, its delicate eco-systems are starting to suffer more and more. One example is Manuel Antonio, which receives several daily flights from San José. Every year, hundreds of thousands of visitors walk the *senderos* in the Manuel Antonio National Park, which measures only 7km², with the result that the monkeys now beg for bananas and the park is closed on Tuesdays so staff can clear all the rubbish. In Tortuguero, tourists are transported across the canals to the lodges and crocodiles by motorboat; a slower form of transport would cause less damage. Furthermore, the criteria for the numerous seals of eco-quality with which hotels and lodges adorn themselves are not always transparent. On the other hand, some eco-lodges – often the small ones – are surprisingly successful with reforestation, giving rise to hope that it is not yet too late for our planet after all.

STONE GIANTS

Hundreds have been discovered so far, and it is assumed that many more are still waiting to be found: manmade stone spheres, in granite and lava, measuring between 10cm and 2m, perfectly rounded and weighing up to an amazing 16 tonnes. They can be found in the south of Costa Rica in the jungle and river estuaries, in valleys and up mountains. The spheres were probably made by the Boruca, a pre-Columbian civilisation, and were possibly intended to symbolise astronomical alignments, as they could be used to "reproduce" them. Many were destroyed by the Spanish, who believed there was gold inside them. Also known as *Indian stone balls*, today they adorn museums, parks and public buildings. There are two in the front garden outside Paseo Colón 2044 in San José. *short.travel/cri5*

ON THE STREET

They await you on roads, in parks and in squares: street-sellers hawking their stocks of sunglasses, watches and water, chewing gum and clothing, souvenirs and perfume. On the Plaza de la Cultura in San José they offer

Stone spheres in the National Museum in San José

pigeon food, although the pigeons there have long been a pest and nuisance. If there is a traffic jam, whether in the city or on a country road, sellers appear almost instantly offering goods through car windows, and the haggling begins. *Ticos* and refugees from Central America, including children and teenagers, try to survive this way. As the police of San José are unable to get the situation under control, they simply confiscate the goods and take them away in lorries.

VOLCANOES - QUITE HARMLESS!

There's no need to worry – volcanic eruptions are rare in Costa Rica, and can usually be predicted in advance. The country's volcanoes also fall short of the popular image in other respects. Not all are in the traditional cone shape, and many are disguised as "ordinary" mountains. The country owes its fertile soil to the volcanic ash. The Arenal Volcano (1,633m), 100km north of San José, is the most active one in the country. In 1968, there was a massive eruption that left more than 80 people dead, and although its eruptions have declined in recent years, no one is allowed to climb to the top. However, there are several hiking trails at the foot of the volcano.

AGRICULTURE

Natural resources are rare, and bananas, coffee, sugar, pineapples, cocoa, palm oil and beef are the country's main export products. The timber industry is also a major economic factor. Costa Rica sells high-grade woods all over the world, but balances the impact with extensive reforesting.

EATING
SHOPPING
SPORT

Feel like Tarzan: take a zip-line through the forest

EATING & DRINKING

Costa Rican cuisine isn't exactly known for its variety or sophistication. It tends to be plain, but tasty. Beans – a source of protein that even makes an ideal breakfast – and maize dishes have played a central role in the local diet for centuries.

THE NATIONAL DISH

Another staple is rice, and the Costa Ricans have hundreds of different ways of preparing it. Rice and black beans are the basic ingredients for the national dish, *casado*. The word actually means "married", and it is said that the dish awaits a *Tico* every day – for the rest of his life – when he marries a *Tica*: rice and fried black beans, often served with scrambled eggs or sour cream, as well as fried plantain, onions, and fried or boiled meat and salad.

Traditionally, the first meal of the day is *gallo pinto*, the second national dish, and again a combination of rice

and black (or red) pan-fried beans, often served with fried or scrambled eggs, sour cream, fried cheese, or thin maize pancakes *(tortillas)*. Ham, chicken or bacon can also be added to the dish.

CAUTION – HOT!

At lunchtime and in the evening, the Costa Ricans appreciate chicken or beef with their rice and beans, and eggs and fish complete the menu. The various vegetable dishes and accompaniments are excellent. Next to carrots, peppers, potatoes, pumpkin and onions, more exotic vegetables such as yucca and cassava roots are also served.

Caution is the watchword when it comes to the apparently innocuous *picadillos* – potatoes, carrots, onions and peppers preserved in chillies and diluted vinegar – which can pack a terrific punch.

Shaken, stirred and often served with rum: refreshing alcoholic mixed drinks

SEAFOOD & CREOLE CUISINE

The sea is one of the country's richest treasures, and provides Costa Ricans with fish and seafood – served in seafood restaurants called *marisquería*. *Ceviche* is a popular starter, consisting of raw fish marinated in lime juice and seasoned with coriander and onions.

Creole cuisine, where coconuts and spices play the main roles, may be less familiar to Europeans. One of the most popular stews is "run down" (also *rondon*), which consists of meat and vegetables cooked in coconut milk.

For dessert there is cheese from Monteverde (such as Monte Rico) or one of many local sweet dishes, such as *granizado con fruta*, ice-cream and fruit on crushed ice.

SALUD!

Popular drinks choices include mixed fruit drinks, such as puréed mango or banana topped up with milk or water *(batidos con leche/agua)*, while hotels also serve pure fruit juices *(frescos)*. Green coconuts *(pipas)*, are sold on the roadside, opened with a machete and the contents slurped through a straw – the perfect thirst-quencher, and also packed with vitamins. Costa Rican coffee is exported all over the world, and the locals drink it all day long.

Costa Ricans greatly appreciate a good beer, and the local varieties – Bavaria, Pilsen and Imperial – are as good as any found in Europe. Wine is usually imported, and while local wines are not bad at all, they are rare and hard to find. Delicious mixed drinks make favourite sundowners, such as *piña colada* (pineapple juice, coconut milk, rum), *daiquirí* (lemon juice, rum, crushed ice), *margarita* (lemon juice, Cointreau, tequila) and *Cuba libre* (white rum, lemon juice, cola).

Guacamole has become a tangy, refreshing classic in Europe too

RESTAURANTS

There are lots of restaurants in San José and the central valley. The middle range is dominated by establishments geared towards US tastes, while more upmarket European restaurants are the preferred choice of well-off locals. In the countryside, you'll find mainly simple pubs *(sodas)* serving local cuisine. Also popular are places that serve an extensive range of pasta and salads, as well as Italian-style pizzas.

In the popular tourist resorts, numerous vegetarian restaurants have sprung up, as well as Italian, French and Asian eateries run by foreigners. Their cooking traditions are now influencing local cuisine, as is fusion-style food from the US.

Menu prices include the mandatory 15 per cent value-added tax. A service charge, normally ten per cent, is usually added on top of that. This is not considered as a tip, however, and staff do appreciate a tip of a maximum of 10 per cent.

ON THE MARKET

All the bigger towns have a central market with lots of food stalls. You sit on stools at the counter to enjoy everything from breakfast to an evening meal, served with coffee and fruit and vegetable juices. You'll find a snack bar on lots of street corners, although the offerings aren't always suitable for delicate stomachs. A *bar* can be almost anything: a pub, somewhere to eat, a café, general stall – or all of the above.

A KITCHEN GODDESS

The star of the Costa Rican cooking scene is Flora Sobrado de Echandi, known all over the country as Tía Florita. Author of almost 20 cookbooks and the star of countless cookery shows *(tiaflorita.tv)*, she demonstrates how the country's traditional cuisine can be varied. Her recipes draw on the tried and tested, but are updated with the use of spices and new ingredients.

TODAY'S SPECIALS

Starters & snacks

CHICHARRONES
Crispy baked pieces of pork crackling

ENCHILADA
Pastry filled with cheese, potatoes
and meat

FRIJOLES MOLIDOS
Mashed beans with onions and peppers

GUACAMOLE
Mashed avocado with lemon juice
and tomatoes

PATACONES
Fried thin slices of plantain

EMPANADA
Maize pancake with beans, cheese,
meat and potatoes

QUESADILLA
Wheat flour tortilla with cheese

SOPA NEGRA
Black bean soup with vegetables
and egg

Main courses

ARROZ CON CARNE
Rice with meat

ARROZ CON PESCADO
Rice with fish

CARNE ASADA
Fried thin slices of beef

GALLO
Tortilla with beans, cheese, meat,
tomatoes and fried potatoes

OLLA DE CARNE
Stew of meat, chicken, potatoes,
vegetables, maize, yucca and plantain

POLLO ASADO
Hot and spicy fried chicken

TAMAL
Maize flatbread filled with meat and
peppers, steamed in banana leaves

Desserts

CAJETA
Dessert made with coconut, vanilla
and milk

CHORREADO
Maize pancake with sour cream

PAN BON
Dark spiced fruit bread

SHOPPING

TICO FASHION

Fashionistas can find brightly embroidered, and often hand-woven, dresses, jackets, blouses and trousers at the markets. Some of these items are made in Guatemala and Mexico, or the designs are inspired by the *molas* embroidery of neighbouring Panama.

DRINKS FROM AN OXCART

In the town of Sarchí and the surrounding area, you will find lots of artisans making colourful *carretas*, the traditional patterned, painted oxcarts that are a symbol of Costa Rica. The carts are made in all possible sizes, and can be used as decorations in homes and gardens, and as minibars. Less striking are the rocking chairs made of leather and wood that collapse for easy transport.

CREATIVE ITEMS FROM NATURE

The ecologically orientated shops in the national parks and their surrounding areas are veritable treasure troves for charming and practical souvenirs. You can buy hand-crafted soaps made from lime oil, mango-fragranced, exotic aromatic oils, writing paper made from banana leaves, children's T-shirts with turtle motifs, and much, much more.

BEAUTY FROM THE RAINFOREST

The rainforest is home to plants that are extremely effective as ingredients for natural tropical cosmetics. The bestseller of Raw Botanicals *(rawbotanic als.com)*, an eco-label from Costa Rica, is Ylang Ylang Miracle: a serum that smooths the skin and is entirely natural.

INSIDER TIP
Anti-ageing from the rainforest

As colourful as the country's fauna and flora: a blanket with *molas* embroidery

BITTER & SWEET

In general, the small coffee fincas produce premium quality beans. Ideally, you can taste and buy when you visit a plantation. Apart from known brands, you can discover great smaller companies, such as *Caribeans Coffee and Chocolate (caribeanschocolate.com)* from Puerto Viejo de Talamanca: they produce organic coffee and delicious chocolate.

MARKET OR CORNER SHOP?

Every village has its *mercado central*, a treasure trove for anything from medicinal herbs and tinctures to shoes, rugs and hand-carved combs. Rural areas are home to numerous *pulperías* – grocer's shops that sell spices and cigarettes, shampoo and milk powder. However, these stands and little shops, which are also known as *pulpe* and *minisúper,* face a growing threat from the major supermarkets.

HANDS OFF!

The black market doesn't only cover tortoiseshell and products made from it, but also sea snails and shells that are protected by CITES, the Convention on International Trade in Endangered Species of Wild Fauna and Flora, created to ensure that international trade doesn't threaten species' survival. As with the purchase of tortoiseshell items, the acquisition of giant shells is damaging: if demand is there these creatures will be caught and killed for tourists. Please do not buy these "souvenirs" or anything made from tortoiseshell or iguana skin. And if you want to buy items made of tropical wood, please be careful to ensure that the wood is grown in plantations, so you don't inadvertently promote the deforestation of ecologically invaluable tropical rainforest.

SPORT & ACTIVITIES

Costa Rica is the perfect destination for sporty nature-lovers. Conditions along the Atlantic and Pacific coasts are excellent for water sports, Costa Rica's national parks are unique, and there are many different and exciting ways to explore them both. You can trek through rainforest, kayak or raft along fast-flowing rivers, ride a horse on a black shimmering lava beach or dive among the turtles and barracudas. Big tour operators here are both trustworthy and safe.

DIVING & SNORKELLING

On the northern end of the Pacific coast, the volcanic Islas Catalinas rise up steeply from the sandy ocean floor to a height of around 30m. Among the sights you'll see diving here are rays, barracudas, sharks, moray eels and turtles. Dive trips to dream-like coral reefs depart from the Playa del Coco and Playa Flamingo. *Deep Blue Diving (Playas del Coco, Guanacaste | tel. 26 70 10 04 | deepblue-diving.com)*, is a good operator, and also runs a PADI diving school where you can get your diving licence. The beaches along the Pacific are also ideal for snorkelling – there are lots of small bays among the rocks between the sandy sections that are home to many fish and crustaceans.

The coral reefs of the Caribbean coast are also suitable for snorkelling, but visibility can be restricted by the surf. The months between September and November are an exception to this – the Caribbean is an absolute dream then.

GOLF

Golf in the Tropics? Particularly appealing here for the diversity of the plant life, say fans. If you play as soon as the sun rises, the climate is pleasant with

In Costa Rica, you can surf on both the Atlantic and Pacific coasts

a lovely light, and you will have only the birds as your companions. The country has a number of golf courses, the loveliest of which is the *Cariari Country Club (18 holes, par 71, 6,260m | clubcariari.com)* at the Meliá Cariari Hotel near Heredia. For information, *see teetimescostarica.com.*

PARAGLIDING

Paragliding has become a very popular way to see Costa Rica from above. There are plenty of cliffs to launch from and landing places on the beach, especially at Caldera and Turrialba. Beginners start with a tandem flight. Circular trips, either as part of a group or as an individual, are offered by *Skyhigh (skyhigh-costarica.com).*

RIDING

Numerous hotels and ranches have suitable mounts, and offer guided hacks around the country. It's best to avoid the poor creatures that spend the whole day in the sun, standing sadly on the beach, and are available for an hourly rate of $10.

RIVER RAFTING

You can do white-water rides in different parts of the country. An experienced skipper guides the inflatable boat over rapids and small waterfalls, and if you're on a multi-day trip you'll stay in a tent beside the river. You can choose from sections of river with different levels of difficulty, as is appropriate for your skills and experience, and there are even suitable tours for children. The most exciting and best-known river for rafting is the Río Pacuare, which flows towards the Caribbean. Day and overnight tours are offered by *Exploradores Outdoors (office in Puerto Viejo de Talamanca | tel. 27 50 20 20 | exploradores outdoors.com).*

STAND-UP PADDLING

Trendy SUP is pretty hip in Costa Rica too. Almost all the windsurfing schools and board shops have the equipment to hire, as do a number of the beach hotels in Uvita and – very often – on the Nicoya Peninsula (for example, at Playa Tamarindo and Playa Sámara). Lessons are available, including in SUP yoga. Why not try it? It's tremendous fun! Available from *Costa Rica Stand up Paddle Adventures (Tamarindo | costaricasupadventures.com).*

SURFING

On the Pacific coast, beginners are advised to try the beach at Sámara, because you can hire the equipment on site and there aren't any dangerous currents. Advanced surfers go to the beaches of Nosara and Tamarindo, or to the Caribbean coast. On that coast, surfers are most frequently seen at Puerto Viejo de Talamanca and Punta Uva.

A highlight is Playa Naranjo in the Santa Rosa National Park on the northwest Pacific coast, because of the huge, right-breaking barrels there between December and April. This spot was made famous by surfer film *The Endless Summer*, and is also known as Roca Bruja, after a huge boulder that breaks the waves. The entry to this part of the enormous and mainly trackless national park is 35km north

INSIDER TIP
Big surf cinema

The Arenal Volcano: with a view like this, this is not your average hike

of Liberia on the Panamericana highway. A tour into this area is a real adventure, for which you will need a 4x4 and to be prepared for no-frills camping in the jungle.

There is greater comfort to be had in the coast's many surf camps, where you will not just find marvellous swells, but also other surfers and backpackers from around the world. The central hub is at Santa Teresa on the southern tip of the Nicoya Peninsula.

TREETOP ADVENTURE

To get that Tarzan feeling amid treehouses and liana vines, try one of the popular *canopy tours*. You'll walk through the treetops in the rainforest using a system of hanging bridges, or glide through the trees on a zip wire. There are now over 100 providers.

The ▶ *Adventure Park (adventure parkcostarica.com)* at the Adventure Park & Hotel Vista Golfo near Puntarenas on the outskirts of a large private forest with views of the Gulf of Nicoya is perfect for a short adventure holiday. As well as 25 zip lines passing over 11 waterfalls, there is a thrilling system of hanging bridges, steps, ladders and ropes that takes you high into the treetops. Horse-riding in the jungle is also offered.

TREKKING

You really must pack your hiking boots, because Costa Rica's species-rich nature is best experienced on foot. Possibilities range from an hour-long stroll through the Manuel Antonio National Park to several days' trekking with local guides through the trackless rainforest, where you'll pitch your own tent for the night. The Corcovado and Rincón de la Vieja national parks provide plenty of eco-friendly adventures and thrills – and have the most species-rich eco-systems in the country. The *Camino de Costa Rica* long-distance hiking trail (280km) crosses the entire country from coast to coast.

WINDSURFING

There are now good lodges for windsurfers at the Laguna de Arenal, with its constant breezes. The neighbouring Lago de Coter also attracts lots of surfers. On the Pacific coast, there are windsurfers on the beaches at Tambor, Flamingo, Potrero and Tamarindo, as well as on the Golfo Dulce.

REGIONAL OVERVIEW

Lago de Nicaragua

NICARAGUA

Laguna Caño Negro

✈ ● Liberia

THE NORTHWEST p. 62

Río San Carlos

Quesada (San Carlos)

Laguna de

Puntarenas

Río Grande de Tárcoles

Dreamy beaches and legendary rainforest

Surfing, diving and plenty of nature

O C É A N O

P A C Í F I C O

O C É A N O

Bahía Chatham

Bahía Wafer

Isla del Coco

P A C Í F I C O

N

2 km
1.24 mi

MAR

CARIBE

Río San Juan

The country's heartland: spectacular nature and a touch of culture

CARIBBEAN COAST p. 92

Reggae vibe in Little Amazonia

CENTRAL PLATEAU p. 40

Alajuela

SAN JOSÉ

Turrialba

Cartago

Puerto Limón

Río Chirripó

Río Telire

San Isidro de El General

PACIFIC COAST p. 78

PANAMÁ

Bahía de Coronado

40 km
24.86 mi

CENTRAL PLATEAU

COLONIAL FLAIR AND NATIONAL PARKS

The Meseta Central (or Valle Central) is the central plateau running down the middle of Costa Rica. Between 1,000m and 1,700m high, it is surrounded by three massifs, with mountains and both active and extinct volcanos. Coffee bushes thrive in the fertile soil, bringing wealth and prosperity to the region.

As well as San José, the modern capital, you will also find lots of traditional Spanish towns full of old-style charm. And San José itself has some of the best museums in the whole of Central America.

Sulphur steam and clouds by the mouth of the crater: bizarre scenery at Poás Volcano

It will only take you an hour to get to the dark beaches of the Pacific Ocean from here. Pleasant, spring-like temperatures – the annual average is 22°C – as well as a tremendous choice of lodges and restaurants, are the appeal and attraction of this lovely landscape for tourists. And with the excellent public transport system, it's easy to reach the volcanoes and nature reserves from San José. Although the area seems rural, with coffee plantations visible as far as the eye can see, it is nevertheless home to over half of all Costa Ricans.

CENTRAL PLATEAU

La Palmera

Santa Rita

La Virgen

Aguas Zarcas

Venecia

Río Cuarto

San Miguel

PROVINCIA
ALAJUELA

PROVINCIA

Tapesco

Bajos del Toro

Palmira

Poás Volcano ★ 6

Varablanca

Zarcero 8

60km, 1½ hrs

San Juanillo

Cirrí Sur

Sabana Redonda

San Pedro

Doka Estate 5

Naranjo

7 Sarchí

San Isidro

Grecia

San Pedro

Roble

San José de
la Montaña

Santa
Bárbara

El Rosario

Carrillos
Bajo

Tambor

San

Barva

San
Rafael

San
Isidr

Candelaria

Tacares

Alajuela
p. 53

Joaquín

San
Antonio

Heredia
p. 49

San José Sur

San

32

Atenas

Garita

10km,
20 mins

San
Juan

Guácima

Río Grande

Turrúcares

27

Pozos

27

Santa Ana

San José
p. 44

Escazú

Picagres

Piedras Negras

Ciudad
Colón

Museo del Oro
Precolombino ★

Alajuelita

Teatro Nacional ★

Grifo Alto

45km, 1 hr

Guayabo

Quitirrisí

Cerros de Escazú

Aserrí

San
Migue

Barbacoas

Santiago

San Rafael

Palmichal

85km, 2¼ hrs

5 km
3.11 mi

PROVINCIA SAN JOSÉ

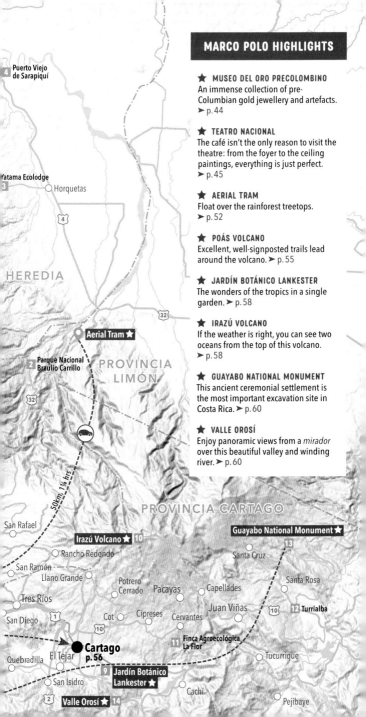

MARCO POLO HIGHLIGHTS

★ **MUSEO DEL ORO PRECOLOMBINO**
An immense collection of pre-Columbian gold jewellery and artefacts.
➤ p. 44

★ **TEATRO NACIONAL**
The café isn't the only reason to visit the theatre: from the foyer to the ceiling paintings, everything is just perfect.
➤ p. 45

★ **AERIAL TRAM**
Float over the rainforest treetops.
➤ p. 52

★ **POÁS VOLCANO**
Excellent, well-signposted trails lead around the volcano. ➤ p. 55

★ **JARDÍN BOTÁNICO LANKESTER**
The wonders of the tropics in a single garden. ➤ p. 58

★ **IRAZÚ VOLCANO**
If the weather is right, you can see two oceans from the top of this volcano.
➤ p. 58

★ **GUAYABO NATIONAL MONUMENT**
This ancient ceremonial settlement is the most important excavation site in Costa Rica. ➤ p. 60

★ **VALLE OROSÍ**
Enjoy panoramic views from a *mirador* over this beautiful valley and winding river. ➤ p. 60

Puerto Viejo de Sarapiquí 4

Yatama Ecolodge 3

Horquetas

HEREDIA

Aerial Tram ★

Parque Nacional Braulio Carrillo 2

PROVINCIA LIMÓN

50 km, 1¼ hrs

PROVINCIA CARTAGO

Guayabo National Monument ★ 13

Santa Cruz

San Rafael

Irazú Volcano ★ 10

Rancho Redondo

Santa Rosa

San Ramón
Llano Grande

Potrero Cerrado Pacayas

Capelládes

Juan Viñas

10 12 Turrialba

Tres Ríos

San Diego

Cot Cipreses Cervantes

11 Finca Agroecológica La Flor

Quebradilla El Tejar

● **Cartago** p. 56

Tucurrique

San Isidro

9 Jardín Botánico Lankester ★

Cachí

Pejibaye

Valle Orosí ★ 14

SAN JOSÉ

(⊞ G–H5) **San José is not a city to fall in love with. With a combination of Spanish planning, modern extensions and a chequerboard road layout, it is dominated by dense traffic.**

The city lies in a coffee-growing valley at a height of 1,150m at the foot of the Cordillera Central, and has a population of around 440,000 (or over 2.1m if you include those in the outlying towns and villages). The upland location means the city has a pleasant climate.

San José has been the capital since 1823, and it's a modern, prosperous metropolis with just a few magnificent buildings and other remnants from the Spanish era. Attempts have been made to add a few spots of colour to an overall grey palette in recent years. The neoclassical Hotel del Rey and the wooden houses from the turn of the last century in the old quarter of Barrio Amón now shine in new splendour, as do the Parque Morazán, Parque de la Merced and Parque Central.

As in many towns and cities in Costa Rica, the *avenidas* run east to west (the odd ones are to the north of the Avenida Central, the evens to the south), the *calles* from north to south (odds to the east of the Calle Central, evens to the west). The city's prettiest area is *Barrio Amón* just north of the centre, with pastel-coloured wooden houses in the Caribbean style and Victorian buildings from the colonial era – perfect for a stroll, during which you will discover plenty of nice cafés and restaurants.

INSIDER TIP **Stress-free city district**

If you intend to stay in the central valley, the two western suburbs of *Escazú* and *Santa Ana (both ⊞ d–e3)* are good choices because while you are outside the metropolis, you are close enough to reach the city centre by bus in only 20 minutes.

WHERE TO START

From the Coca Cola bus terminal it's a 1.5km walk along the Avenida Central to the **Plaza de la Cultura** *(⊞ d–e3)*. Taxis should not charge more than 1,300 colón ($2.50). On the Plaza you will find an ICT Tourist Information Centre, the gold museum and the Teatro Nacional. If you fancy a break, head to the café there, or go and sit under the arcades of the Gran Hotel. The Avenida Central continues to the National Museum.

SIGHTSEEING

MUSEO DEL ORO PRECOLOMBINO ★ ⚘

The treasure is in the cellar: the hoard of gold in the underground museum complex of the Banco Central is not only of inestimable value, but is also fascinating and beautiful. Tiny frogs, birds and crocodiles, thousands of years old and made of pure gold; little, highly detailed dancers and shamans; fabulous necklaces, bracelets, plates and goblets – the 1,600 items on display date back to between 500 BCE and the 16th century. The museum's treasures alone make a visit to the capital worthwhile! *Daily 9.15am–4.30pm | C/ 5/Av. Central, below the Plaza de la Cultura | museosdelbancocentral.org | ⏱ 2 hrs | ▥ d–e3*

TEATRO NACIONAL ★

The neo-Renaissance theatre, built in 1897, was based on the Paris Opera, and with its marble staircases and frescoes, gilded foyer and Venetian mirrors, it is the loveliest theatre in Central America. The ceiling painting in the entrance hall can be seen on the five-colon note. The auditorium, which tilts towards the stage, is levelled for dance performances. For 3,500 colones you can take an exciting guided tour: the young guides show you details which you would never discover on your own, such as "errors" in the fresco that were included intentionally. The most beautiful place in San José for relaxing with a cup of tea or a *latte macchiato* is the magnificent 🛆 *Alma de Café (Mon–Sat 9am–7pm, Sun 9am–6pm)* in the Belle Époque style. *Daily 9am–5pm, guided tours until 4pm | C/ 3–5/Av. 2 | teatronacional.go.cr | ▥ d–e3*

INSIDER TIP
Hidden secrets

MUSEO NACIONAL DEL JADE

You won't see a larger exhibition of pre-Columbian excavated items, stones and figures made of jade anywhere else. Even though public opinion of the new building, which

Museo Nacional del Jade: jewellery and ceramics from the pre-Columbian era

cost more than $20m and looks like a chunk of uncut jade, is on the negative side, the inside is worth seeing. The lights are dimmed, and over its five floors you are immersed in the whole world of this stone that was once valued all over Central America for its use in ritual practices. The little 🐗 sculptures by local artist Olger Villegas Cruz in the entrance hall (admission free) look surprisingly alive. *Daily 8am–5pm | Plaza de la Democracia (C/ 13/Av. Central) | museo deljade.grupoins.com| ⊙ 2½ hrs | 🔲 e3*

MUSEO NACIONAL 😺 🚩

Typical for Costa Rica. The tour of the National Museum starts in a butterfly house full of palm trees and tropical flowers. There's flapping and buzzing all around. It is interesting as you continue: you can see the Nobel Peace Prize awarded to Óscar Arias Sánchez in 1987, as well as the office and original furniture of former presidents. The roof garden with frangipani trees and benches to sit on is fabulous – perfect for a rest. *Tue–Sat 8.30am–4.30pm, Sun 9am–4.30pm | Plaza de la Democracia (C/ 15/Av. Central–2) | museocostarica.go.cr| ⊙ 2½ hrs | 🔲 e3*

PARQUE NACIONAL

There is an eye-catching bronze monument from 1885 in a central location in the middle of this park that marks the abolition of slavery and the fact that five Central American states resisted William Walker's attempts at annexation. *C/ 15–19/Av. 1–3 | 🔲 e–f3*

MUSEO DE ARTE Y DISEÑO CONTEMPORÁNEO

One of the few old buildings in the capital is home to the biggest and best exhibition of contemporary art and design. There are also temporary exhibitions on topics such as fashion design and graphic design – 🐖 and free admission on Mondays. *Mon–Sat 9.30am–4.55pm | C/ 15/Av. 3 | madc. cr| ⊙ 1 hr | 🔲 e3*

PARQUE ZOOLÓGICO SIMÓN BOLÍVAR 😺

A visit to the zoo in Costa Rica, where there are so many wild animals to see? The large verdant park, with tropical trees and a lake, is actually more reminiscent of a botanical garden – a refreshing antidote when you need a break from city life. Apart from the jaguars and turtles, the *Ticos* are most fascinated by the boa constrictors. *Daily 9am–4.30pm | C/ 9/Av. 11 | fundazoo.org | ⏱ 1–2 hrs | 🗺 e2*

SPIROGYRA BUTTERFLY GARDEN (JARDÍN DE MARIPOSAS) 😺

As it is a little smaller than the other butterfly farms in the country – although every bit as diverse – the Butterfly Garden in the capital is perfect for visiting with children. *Mon–Thu 9am–1pm, Fri–Sun 9am–2pm | C/ 11 | San Francisco de Goicoechea | butter flygardencostarica.com | 🗺 e2*

MUSEO DE LOS NIÑOS 😺

The interactive children's museum offers many varied attractions and activities in its 33 rooms and outside space. Children will experience a dairy farm and an earthquake, and learn how an orchestra and space travel work. *Tue–Fri 8.30am–4.30pm, Sat/ Sun 9am–5pm | C/ 4/Av. 9 | museo. museocr.org | ⏱ 1 hr | 🗺 d2*

EATING & DRINKING

11-47

Fusion cuisine with a friendly and cosy atmosphere. While the menu is rather limited, the dishes are beautifully put together. Great tasting menus with matching wines. *C/ 19/Av. 11–13 | tel. 22 56 18 25 | hotelaranjuez.com | $$–$$$ | 🗺 f2*

DORIS METROPOLITAN

The Doris specialises in meat that is prepared using the dry-aged method. You can watch the process and staff can explain how it works. Excellent service, and a huge selection of drinks. *C/ 1, between Av. 1 and 3 | Santa Ana, 14km west of San José | tel. 22 82 22 21 | dorismetropolitan.com/ costa-rica | $$–$$$ | 🗺 G5*

LA ESQUINA DE BUENOS AIRES

Excellent restaurant and Argentinian-style grill – with large servings and great meat, although they also have a comprehensive vegetarian menu. *C/ 11/Av. 4 | tel. 22 23 19 09 | laesquina debuenosaires.net | $$$ | 🗺 e3*

SODA TAPIA

For 80 years *gallo pinto* has been served at this place in La Sabana district near the Museum of Art. It's lively, and it occasionally gets loud on the roadside terrace, but that's what's charming about this iconic restaurant, which opens daily from 6am. *C/ 42/Av. 2 | tel. 22 22 67 34 | $ | 🗺 a3*

TIN JO

Asian cuisine: Indian and Thai curries, fish specialities and seafood, plus lots of vegetarian dishes. There is also an extensive wine list. *C/ 11/Av. 6–8 | tel. 22 21 76 05 | tinjo.com | $$ | 🗺 e3–4*

SHOPPING

As a general rule, many of the goods on offer in the capital's markets and craft stores are from Guatemala and South America. However, there are also some pretty, typically Costa Rican products. One treasure trove – especially at weekends – is the *Plaza de la Cultura*, with ⚑ stands at which potential customers haggle for hammocks, ceramics, wood carvings and leather goods. Outside the National Museum on the *Plaza de la Democracia*, small stands sell woven goods from Guatemala, and silver and ceramics from Mexico.

MULTIPLAZA ESCAZÚ

This mall is the biggest in Central America: a huge complex with more than 400 shops, banks and a few exquisite restaurants. Obviously, all the known fast-food chains have outlets here as well. This place is ideal for starting your holiday because you can do your shopping, get cash, phone cards, medicine, and so on – all in one go. *Mon–Sat 10am–9pm, Sun until 8pm | San Rafael de Escazú, 8km outside the capital, on the 27 | multiplaza.com/escazu | ▥ G5*

NIGHTLIFE

The *Barrio La California*, known as La Cali, adjoins the Parque Nacional to the southeast. Students and other young people come here to party, especially on weekends. You'll find cool bars and pubs featuring trendy bands. Nice places include the *El Cuartel de la Boca del Monte (Av. 1/C 21–23 | FB)* and the iconic *La Cali bar (Thu–Sat from 7pm | Av. Central/C 21–23 | FB)*.

AROUND SAN JOSÉ

🔢 CERROS DE ESCAZÚ

By bus to Matinilla, from there a 10km / 3–5hr hike to Bebedero

San José is surrounded by mountains – and this strenuous hike takes you to the *Cerros de Escazú* range, whose peaks are visible on clear days. Set off at 7am from San José by bus to Matinilla via Santa Ana (bus no. 9; if you can only get to Salitral, that will also work, although it will be more tiring). This is the starting point of an unmarked high-altitude trail in an easterly direction up onto the Cerros de Escazú. You really can't miss this trail, and the view is mostly clear; navigation aids will work here. It is recommended that you set off early because there is quite a height difference to conquer. The start is at 900m and the highest point is at 1,300m, with the route including uphill and downhill legs. The trail finishes in Bebedero, where you find the perfect end of your hike at the *Mirador Tiquicia ($$)*. Here you can enjoy traditional food and folklore entertainment, with far-ranging views. Bus no.9, which run every 15 to 20 minutes, will take you back to San José. ▥ G5

HEREDIA

(□ G5) **Only 10km north of San José, and yet an entirely different world. Heredia scores with its balanced climate, colonial architecture and delightful small-town atmosphere.**

The capital (population 140,000) of the province of the same name is known locally as Ciudad de Flores, the "City of Flowers". At a height of 1,137m, it gets its name from its spring-like temperatures, the containers of flowers outside the houses and the abundance of floral decorations. The tiled roofs of the white houses are dominated by the domes of the churches. Massive wooden doors and thick walls keep the heat out and the houses cool, screening patios and gardens from view. The local industry is coffee. East of the centre is the national university, and its students lend a youthful atmosphere to the city. Heredia's layout is strictly colonial. It was founded by the Spanish, who came here from former capital Cartago in the first half of the 18th century.

Almost more embrasures than bricks: El Fortín in Heredia

SIGHTSEEING

PARQUE CENTRAL

Mansions in the colonial and neoclassical style, once the residences of coffee barons, are grouped around this park, the green heart of the city. On the northwest corner is the embellished post office, on the east side the vast 18th-century church *Parroquia Inmaculada Concepción*: the thick stone walls and 30 supporting pillars of the nave ensure that it's earthquake-proof. The city administration is housed in parts of the Spanish fortress on the northern side, which includes the *El Fortín* tower from 1876 with its embrasures (holes through which cannons could be fired). The townhouse of former President Alfredo González Flores on the square's northeast corner, *Casa de la Cultura (casadelacultura alfredogonzalezflores.blogspot.com)*, is now used as offices and a cultural centre hosting exhibitions and events.

MUSEO DE BIOLOGÍA MARINA

The university's institute of marine biology has a museum with around 2,000 exhibits of flora and fauna from the country's oceans. *Mon–Fri 8am–5pm | Universidad Nacional (eastern end of Av. Central) | ⏱ 90 mins*

FINCA CAFÉ BRITT

Heredia is all about coffee! The town is surrounded by plantations, and this coffee *finca* is one of the best-known in the country. They run an entertaining hour-and-a-half tour where you'll discover how gourmet coffee is made, and why there are huge tropical trees growing beside the coffee bushes. The coffee factory, which dates back to the 19th century, is 2km north of the town

INSIDER TIP
Learn about coffee

centre. Today it also sells cocoa and nuts; you can try and buy them in the restaurant and shop *(daily 8am–5pm). Tours daily 9am, 11am and 3.15pm | Mercedes Norte de Heredia | coffee-tour.com*

MUSEO DE CULTURA POPULAR

A restored country house (1885) that illustrates rural life at the end of the 19th century. At the entrance are a vast stone oven and a stone tub for grinding coffee. Nearby, traditional restaurant *La Fonda ($)* serves local cuisine cooked by women from Heredia on Sundays. *Mon–Fri 7am–noon, 1–4pm | Santa Lucía de Barva (3km north between Heredia and Barva de Heredia, 1.2km off the main road) | museo.una.ac.cr | ⏱ 1 hr*

INSIDER TIP
Sunday lunch

What a beak! A toucan in the Braulio Carrillo National Park

EATING & DRINKING

L'ANTICA ROMA

SIDER TIP
Strawberry heaven!

Pasta al forno or a traditional stone-baked pizza? Accompanied by an excellent house wine, and to finish, the home-made strawberry cheesecake. *¡Muy rico! Av. 7/C/ 7 | tel. 22 62 90 73 | $$*

KAWAH CAFÉ

Lovely meeting place for breakfast: home-made lemonade, fruit juices, bowls and pancakes. Delicious soups and generous salads at lunchtime, too. *N 111/C. 32 (opposite the southern entrance of the Mall Oxígeno) | tel. 22 63 37 37 | kawah.cr | $$*

EL TIGRE VESTIDO

The restaurant at the wonderful country estate *Finca Rosa Blanca*, 5km to the northwest in *Santa Bárbara de Heredia*, serves excellent dinner. They grow the organic ingredients themselves, and meals are accompanied by the best table wines. Booking recommended. *Tel. 22 69 95 55 | eltigre vestido.com | $$$*

SHOPPING

PASEO DE LAS FLORES

Two-storey shopping mall with over 300 shops, plus self-service restaurants and nice cafés. *Mon–Sat 11am–7pm, Sun 11am–8pm | C/ Cordero | paseodelasflores.com*

NIGHTLIFE

🐾 Listen to marimba music and several open-air concerts a week in the *pavilion* in the *Parque Central*. People, including lots of students, meet in the bars on the west side of the university.

AROUND HEREDIA

2 PARQUE NACIONAL BRAULIO CARRILLO

45km to the Aerial Tram northeast of Heredia / 1 hr 10 mins on the N112 and N32

Steep mountains, gorges, impenetrable rainforest and steaming cloud forest: the largely undeveloped *national park (daily 8am–3.30pm)* north of Hereida was created in 1978 when the road from San José to Puerto Limón was built through it. The rainforest, home to 100 orchid varieties, is also a habitat for jaguars and ocelots, tapirs and monkeys, colourful parrots, toucans and shy quetzals. Rivers and waterfalls abound, and the distinctive red flowers of large *llama del bosque* trees glow. This is where the volcanoes Barva (2,906m, several crater lakes) and *Cacho Negro* are located. Access to Barva is via the San José de la Montaña to Sacramento road; from there it's a 5km signposted hike. **INSIDER TIP** **Spot countless animals** Take a guide because they are trained to spot animals which are very difficult to see otherwise. The main entrance, *Zurquí* (with a cafeteria and guide service), is on the N32 between San José and Guápiles, past the Zurquí Tunnel.

Also on the N32, 5km after the Río Sucio, a 3km forest track to the right leads to the legendary ★ 👓 *Aerial Tram (daily 8am–4pm | rainforest adventure.com)*, a gondola lift that takes you 1,300m into the rainforest and back in an hour and a half with many stops. Beforehand, a video shows you what to expect, although the reality is much more exciting! In addition to the gondola ride, you can book a bird-watching tour, a visit to the serpentarium, the butterfly garden and the 🚩 frog garden, home to the lucky *blue jeans dart frog* (or strawberry poison-dart frog). Also available is a canopy tour with seven zip lines and various trekking tours. If you only want to go to the Aerial Tram, you can take the bus from Heredia to Guápiles or Puerto Viejo de Sarapiquí *(hourly from C/ 12/Av. 7–9)* to the bus stop 27km after the Zurquí tunnel.

A second entrance to the national park is located in the heights of the cloud forest at the Barva volcano. ▢ *H4*

🟥 YATAMA ECOLODGE
75km northeast of Heredia / 2 hrs on the N112, N32 and N4

The Yatama Ecolodge is located on the northeastern border of the Braulio Carrillo National Park at a junction of the road to Puerto Viejo (access from Las Horquetas). Here, Pedro Mendez Tam has achieved the almost unimaginable: he is expanding the national park on his own initiative, carrying out

intensive reforestation and has already "donated" 40 hectares of his private forest to the park over the past 12 years. With the help of German environmental protection organisations Grimm and Tropica Verde, he is adding another 220 hectares to the nature reserve. An impressive project that you should visit! An immense natural world has established itself in the tangle of orchids, lianas, mosses and ferns, home to snakes, frogs, insects and birds. It's best to plan at least two days in the jungle because there's

INSIDER TIP
Take time for nature

so much stunning nature to take in. Booking is required because the journey is complicated and needs to be well coordinated. *Tel. 70 15 11 21 | FB: Yatama Ecolodge Sarapiqui | ▢ H4*

🟥 PUERTO VIEJO DE SARAPIQUÍ
82km northeast of Heredia / 1¾ hrs on the N112, N32 and N4

To the north of Heredia is a road that follows the Braulio Carrillo National Park through some of Costa Rica's most diverse landscapes and mountain regions to this once-important port on the Rio Sarapiquí, which is connected to the Rio Colorado by the Río San Juan. This means that Barra del Colorado and Tortuguero national parks are also accessible from Puerto Viejo by boat.

Today, the town is somewhat sleepy, and only comes alive in the evenings, when young people meet in the cheap *sodas* and around the football pitch in the centre. Visitors tend to head for the small harbour at the end of town: several operators there offer

Glide through the treetops in a steel cage: Aerial Tram in the Braulio Carrillo National Park

boat trips on the rivers in the area, as well as rafting tours over the rapids of the Río Sarapiquí. There are many eco-lodges in all price ranges in the area. *H3*

ALAJUELA

(G5) **The altitude (950m) of the capital of the province of the same name ensures a spring-like climate all year round, something that the city's 276,000 inhabitants appreciate as much as visitors from the rest of the plateau.**

Alajuela's pleasant atmosphere and convenient location close to the international airport is also increasingly appreciated by tourists. The country's second-biggest city developed from a tiny church built by the Spanish in 1782. It is the birthplace of national hero Juan Santamaría. A large bronze memorial to him has been erected in the eponymous park south of the Parque Central.

SIGHTSEEING

PARQUE CENTRAL
Shaded by tall, dense mango trees and several impressive palm trees, this

Award-winning coffee beans thrive on the slopes of the Poás Volcano

park marks the centre of the city. Most of the other sights are within walking distance of it. On the west side *(C/ 2)* are the National Bank and the building where the country's parliament first met in 1824. On the east side is the snowy-white *cathedral*, dating from the turn of the last century, which has a vast corrugated metal dome.

MUSEO HISTÓRICO CULTURAL JUAN SANTAMARÍA 🐖

A lavish building in the colonial style (north of the Parque Central) documents the battles between the US army of mercenaries under William Walker and the bold actions of the Costa Rican national hero. Pretty patio. *Tue–Sun 9am–5pm | C/ 2 Obispo Tristán/Av. 1 | museojuansantamaria. go.cr |* ⏱ *30–45 mins*

EATING & DRINKING

Calle 1 in the centre is full of *sodas* and mid-range restaurants.

MERCADO MUNICIPAL

The juice of the *guanábana* tastes great! You can get a glass at the stalls of the Mercado

INSIDER TIP
Have a glass of guanábana

Municipal, two blocks west of the central park, where you can also sample the region's food specialities. *Mon–Sat 6am–6pm*

EL MIRADOR DE ALAJUELA

A vast sea of lights. Come to Pilas, about 6km to the north of Alajuela, in the evening to enjoy the panoramic views of the twinkling lights of San José and the surrounding villages. The food? Typical *Tico* cuisine with huge portions. *N712, on the road to Poás Volcano | Pilas | tel. 24 41 93 47 | restauranteelmiradordealajuela.com | $$*

PESQUERÍA DA LIMONTA

Excellent fish cuisine with an Italian touch. From ceviche and risotto to seafood-stuffed ravioli and panna cotta with an orange sauce: everything is superb! *C/ 5/Av. 6 | tel. 24 30 35 72 | FB | $$*

SHOPPING

FERIA DEL AGRICULTOR

The weekly market for fruit and vegetables, meat and fish is supplied by small and organic farmers, and also sells clothing, souvenirs and crafts.

Fri noon–8pm, Sat 5.30am–2pm | Plaza de Ferias/Av. 4 Concordia | Facebook: Plaza Ferias Alajuela

AROUND ALAJUELA

5 DOKA ESTATE 🌂

12km north of Alajuela / 25 mins on the N712 and via Sabanilla

For almost 100 years, the Vargas Ruíz family has owned this coffee farm on the slopes of the Poás Volcano, where they produce multiple-award-winning coffees. The roasting machine is a listed architectural monument, still used today and included in a guided tour. A pleasant highlight at the end is the *coffee tasting*, where you can also enjoy the family's own chocolates. *Mon–Fri 8am–3.30pm, Sat/Sun 8am–2.30pm, tours daily 8am, 9am, 10am, 11am, noon, 1.30pm and 2.30pm | tel. 24 49 51 52 | dokaestate.com |* ⏱ *2 hrs |* 🗺 *G5*

6 POÁS VOLCANO ⭐ 🚩

30km north of Alajuela Poás / 50 mins on the N712

Poás made its presence felt in late 2019, when it briefly erupted and spewed sulphur. It has calmed down now, although the access road can still be closed again at any time. The road winds past coffee plantations and up to the national park at a height of 2,705m. Set off for the volcano after an early breakfast (don't forget to take a jacket!), because clouds usually start to roll in during the morning, impairing the view of the massive 1.5km-diameter main crater. Sulphurous vapours usually rise from the turquoise waters of the lagoon. Then follow a jungle path, which branches off just before the crater and is flanked by bromeliads and huge tree ferns, to the *Laguna Botos*, the crater of a volcano that became extinct several thousand years ago and is now a deep-blue lake. As an alternative to

Bronze statue of national hero Juan Santamaría in his hometown of Alajuela

the expensive Poás restaurant, there are two small restaurants with fabulous views and good prices a few kilometres below the entrance to the park. *Daily 8am–4pm | book tickets to the park online at sinac.go.cr |* ⏲ *½ day | ▢ G4*

7 SARCHÍ
27km northwest of Alajuela / 1 hr on the N118

The legendary craft centre is famous for its hand-painted, brightly coloured oxcarts *(carretas pintadas)*, which were once used to transport coffee and are now a national cultural icon, having been added to the UNESCO Intangible Cultural Heritage of Humanity list. There are lots of souvenir and arts and crafts shops, plus restaurants and cafés, in the small town. Have a look at the many historic, painted wooden wheels on display in the Joaquín Chaverri *Fabrica de Carretas* (Oxcart Factory), founded in 1902 and with a particularly large and colourful range of carts. In Sarchí Norte is the vast *Jardin Botánico Else Kientzler (daily 8am–4pm | elsegarden.com),* with some 2,000 tropical plants – and the perfect spot for a picnic. ▢ *G5*

INSIDER TIP
Inspirational oxcart wheels

8 ZARCERO
50km northwest of Alajuela / 1 hr 20 mins via Sarchí

From Sarchí, head northwest to arrive at Zarcero, at an altitude of 1,700m. The surrounding mountains enhance the town's beauty, and the year-round spring-like temperatures and clean air are further attractions. In the *Parque Evangelista Blanco Brenes* outside the church, an artist has trimmed cypress trees into over-sized fantasy shapes and figures *(topiarios)* – animals, but also helicopters and other objects. Excellent meals are served in the *Rancho de Ceci* restaurant *(daily until 8pm | tel. 24 63 33 44 | $$)* 2km north of the town in Laguna. ▢ *F4*

CARTAGO

(▢ H5) **Cartago, the former capital and the oldest city in the country, has often been challenged by fate: destroyed by six earthquakes (the worst ones were in 1841 and 1910), and threatened by eruptions from the Irazú Volcano and by flooding.**

And yet, time and again, Cartago has been rebuilt. Established by the Spanish in 1563, it was the nation's capital until 1823. Today, the "old city" has an entirely new look, because all of the buildings are from the 20th century. Cartago (population 30,000) is 22km southeast of San José, at a height of 1,440m, so it is a little cooler here. Mountains and fertile plains surround the city, but a number of factories are also dotted around the green landscape.

SIGHTSEEING

RUINAS DE LA PARROQUIA
Only the external walls of the cathedral were spared by the devastating earthquake of 1910; since then, the

The eponymous angels watch over the Basílica de Nuestra Señora de Los Ángeles

vast structure, constructed of granite in 1575, has been a ruin. The garden on the inside is open to visitors. *Parque Central*

MUSEO MUNICIPAL DE CARTAGO 🐗

Museum (admission free) exhibiting contemporary art by creative people from the surrounding area. Some of the works on display are really interesting. *Daily 9am–4pm | Av. 3/C/0 | ⏱ 45 mins*

BASÍLICA DE LOS ÁNGELES

Huge white figures of angels watch over the main entrance. On 2 August the church, which was rebuilt in 1926 in the Byzantine style and is home to a shrine to the Virgin Mary, is the venue for a festival and procession, to which thousands of people travel from all over the country. In 2023, the procession is said to have attracted two million visitors. There are numerous display cabinets inside the church, and the faithful make votive offerings in the form of miniature versions of their ailing organs and pray for healing. *Av. Central/C/ 13–15 A | santuarionacional.org*

EATING & DRINKING

LA PUERTA DEL SOL

Typical *soda* with a bar. It's very busy from morning until night with the television on continuously – so ideal for checking out the local colour. Order *casado con pollo*, but the vegetarian dishes with grilled cheese are equally delicious and the servings very generous. *Av. 1/C/ 13 C (on the north side of the basilica) | tel. 25 51 06 15 | $*

SHOPPING

MERCADO MUNICIPAL

The market sells souvenirs and crafts such as ceramics and leather goods as well as food. *Mon–Sat 6am–5.30pm, Sun 6am–noon | Av. 1–3/C/ 2–4*

AROUND CARTAGO

9 JARDÍN BOTÁNICO LANKESTER ★
5km southeast of Cartago / 10 mins on the N10

This botanical garden in a large park, which was created in the 1940s, is a must for orchid-lovers. Some of the over 750 varieties flower in the greenhouse. There are also 40 types of bamboo, a large cactus garden, and countless migratory birds in winter. The garden has been extended to include a Japanese garden with bamboos, a pond and a bridge. An excellent time to visit is in March or April, when many of the orchids are in flower. *Daily 8.30am–4.30pm | jbl.ucr.ac.cr | ○ 3 hrs | ▥ H5*

10 IRAZÚ VOLCANO ★
30km north of Cartago / 50 mins on the N219

The wind is bitterly cold at the rim of the crater of Irazú (3,432m). But the views over the countryside, of rich fields and small settlements, are exceptional. On clear days during the dry season (and only then), you can see two of the world's oceans at the

Just one of more than 750 species: an orchid in the Jardín Botánico Lankester

same time – the coastline of the Gulf of Nicoya (Pacific) on one side, and the Caribbean coast of the Atlantic on the other. And Lake Nicaragua sparkles to the north. During the approach to the volcano, there are lovely views of the mountain landscape of the Valle Central, with its potato and strawberry fields, oak groves and – not unusual in this area – herds of speckled Holstein dairy cows.

The vegetation stops shortly after you enter the *national park (daily 8am–3.30pm)*, leaving the area looking uncannily like the moon – as Neil Armstrong himself once said on a visit. The ground is covered in fine, grey volcanic sand. Looking down 300m into the main crater, which measures 1,000m in diameter, is extremely impressive, even if the apple-green acid lake only contains water during the rainy season. If you walk north around the main crater, you'll come across several fumaroles (vents in the earth where volcanic gases escape). To the northeast is the Turrialba Volcano, and down in the valley to the west lies San José. Occasionally the Barva Volcano will appear out of the clouds. On the way back you can enjoy a typical *gallo pinto* in various restaurants, served with fried bananas. Admire the pictures of the 1910 eruption at the stylish *Restaurante 1910 (tel. 25 63 60 63 | restaurante1910.com | $$)* at the end of the village of *Cot*. They serve exceptionally good food on two glazed terraces. The sea bass *(corvina)* with

SIDER TIP
Café con leche and a volcanic eruption

vegetables, baked bananas and brown rice is particularly popular. ⌘ *H5*

⑪ FINCA AGROECOLÓGICA LA FLOR

17km east of Cartago / 30 mins on the N230 and N10

Everyone who works at this beautiful, ecologically orientated, non-profit finca shows great dedication. It's a great place to take a Spanish course, meet interesting people from all over the world and integrate into farm life (participation is encouraged!). There are also excursions and yoga courses. Here you have the rare opportunity to work as a volunteer without having to book in advance. *La Flor de Paraíso | tel. 25 34 80 03 | fincalaflor.org*

INSIDER TIP
Volunteer – no need to book

⑫ TURRIALBA

40km east of Cartago / 1 hr 10 mins on the N10

The town of 30,000 inhabitants is perched at an altitude of 625m in the hills approaching the 3,339m-high Turrialba Volcano on the river of the same name. White water-rafting fans, visitors to the volcano and those interested in archaeology meet here on the way to Guayabo. Numerous providers undercut each other with favourable prices for rafting tours; multi-day packages are also on offer. There is a large selection of beautiful lodges and inexpensive guesthouses, the best of which are located on the river and often offer kayaking tours. ⌘ *J5*

White water rafting near Turrialba

13 GUAYABO NATIONAL MONUMENT ★

40km north-east of Cartago / 1¼ hrs on the N230

In an exceptional setting in the foothills of the Guayabo volcano lies this pre-Columbian excavation site, the most significant archaeological site in the country and a national monument. Guayabo was discovered back in the 19th century, but wasn't excavated until the end of the 1960s. Roads, burial mounds, aqueducts and foundations all indicate that a settlement flourished here between CE 800 and 1400, but that the site was already inhabited by 500 BCE. Art and ritual objects made of ceramic, jade, gold and semi-precious stones all provide information on the cultural and religious significance of the place.

So far, only a small area measuring approximately 200m by 100m of a more-than-2km² ceremonial site has been reclaimed from the jungle. Paved tracks open up the surrounding rainforest. There are wonderful panoramic views from the *mirador*. Animal and plant-lovers enjoy the site's unspoilt flora and fauna. There is a map of the trails and excavation finds at the entrance to Guayabo, which is surrounded by dense forest. *Daily 8am–3.30pm | ⌖ J5*

14 VALLE OROSÍ ★

18km to Orosí southeast of Cartago / 30 mins on the N10 and N224

Travel on an idyllic route through *Paraíso*, driving through vast coffee plantations to a valley that is irrigated by the Río Grande de Orosí. Even the

Spanish loved this area: the Franciscans built the small *mission church of San José* in Orosí in 1735. The white bell tower stands next to the main building, with its flat, tiled, gabled roof. The *Mirador Orosí* viewpoint in the village offers lovely vistas over the charming valley.

On the way from Orosí, following the river and lake and about 10km past Cachí, is the 🔊 *Casa del Soñador* (The House of the Dreamer), a woodwork studio. The artisans here are totally committed to their craft: take a look at the details brothers Hermes and Miguel Quesada have carved into the wood!

After crossing the high dam on the eastern shore of the lake, on the way back to Paraíso you'll come to *Ujarrás*, with the remains of a colonial *church*

WHERE TO STAY ON THE CENTRAL PLATEAU

IN THE MIDST OF NATURE

The *Peace Lodge (18 rooms | La Paz Waterfall Gardens Nature Park | Vara Blanca | tel. 24 82 21 00 | waterfall gardens.com | $$$)* is located near the beautiful Poás Volcano at an altitude of 1,500m. The park includes the amazing *La Paz* waterfall, which you can hike to through the cloud forest. Ideal for a relaxing stay: the rooms, designed with lots of wood and natural stone, have rain showers, a whirlpool and a fireplace.

THE PERFECT START

To make you feel good: the *Posada Nena (Av. 7 | between C/ 2 and 4 | Santa Ana | tel. 22 82 11 73 | posadanena.com | $$)*, owned by MARCO POLO author Volker Alsen, is located in Santa Ana and has 11 cosy rooms set around a garden. You'll experience that Costa Rican holiday feeling here right from the start. You can also get lots of information and tips, a phone card or simply a tropical cocktail.

built at the end of the 17th century. Nearby, some old plantation buildings were at risk of collapsing, and are now maintained by the Costa Rican tourist office. It's a great spot for a picnic. *H–J 5–6*

THE
NORTHWEST

COWBOY LIVING AND TROPICAL BEACHES

Farms, zebu cattle and *sabaneros* – Central American cowboys – combine to create a picture of Costa Rica's "Wild West" and Pacific coast. The Northwest is hot and dry. Its vast, parched plains are reminiscent of African savannah, the only shade provided by umbrella-like trees. The only rain worth mentioning falls from May to November, and turns the land a fresh green.

People here make their living from cattle breeding, and much of the land is pasture and grassland. Tourism is another main source of

Suspension bridge in the rainforest – for those with a head for heights!

income: the Northwest, consisting of the province of Guanacaste and parts of Puntarenas, is one of the country's best-developed regions, with direct flights to Liberia Airport from both Europe and the US.

The region has over a dozen national parks and reservations, with tropical dry forests and rainforests in the low plains and mist-enshrouded cloud forest in higher regions. Turtles appreciate the still largely empty Pacific coast as a breeding ground.

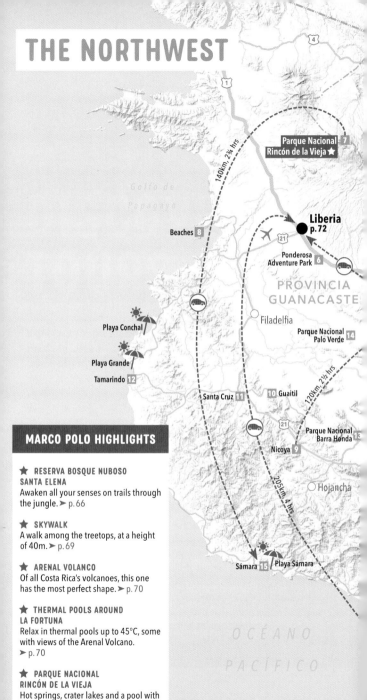

THE NORTHWEST

Parque Nacional **7**
Rincón de la Vieja ★

140km, 2¾ hrs

Golfo de
Papagayo

Liberia
p.72

Beaches **8**

Ponderosa
Adventure Park **6**

PROVINCIA
GUANACASTE

Playa Conchal

Filadelfia

Parque Nacional **14**
Palo Verde

Playa Grande

Tamarindo **12**

Santa Cruz **11**

10 Guaitil

120km, 2½ hrs

Parque Nacional
Barra Honda **13**

Nicoya **9**

MARCO POLO HIGHLIGHTS

★ **RESERVA BOSQUE NUBOSO
SANTA ELENA**
Awaken all your senses on trails through
the jungle. ➤ p.66

★ **SKYWALK**
A walk among the treetops, at a height
of 40m. ➤ p.69

★ **ARENAL VOLANCO**
Of all Costa Rica's volcanoes, this one
has the most perfect shape. ➤ p.70

★ **THERMAL POOLS AROUND
LA FORTUNA**
Relax in thermal pools up to 45°C, some
with views of the Arenal Volcano.
➤ p.70

★ **PARQUE NACIONAL
RINCÓN DE LA VIEJA**
Hot springs, crater lakes and a pool with
health-giving volcanic mud. ➤ p.73

○ Hojancha

205km, 4 hrs

Sámara **15** Playa Sámara

OCÉANO

PACÍFICO

NICARAGUA

COSTA RICA

Lago de
Nicaragua

Río San Juan

Los Chiles

Upala

PROVINCIA
ALAJUELA

San Rafael

Arenal Volcano ★

1 **Thermal pools around
La Fortuna ★**

Místico Park **2**

5 Ecocentro Danaus

Laguna de Arenal
P. 70

Tilarán

3 **Arenal Natura
Ecological Park**

Butterfly Conservatory **4**

Cañas

50km, 1¾ hrs

115km, 2½ hrs

Ciudad
Quesada

Skywalk ★

● **Monteverde**
p.66

Las Juntas

**Reserva Bosque
Nuboso Santa Elena
(Santa Elena Cloud
Forest Reserve) ★**

Zarcero

Miramar

San Ramón

PROVINCIA PUNTARENAS

Espíritu
Santo

Palmares

Puntarenas

San Mateo

Orotina

Península de Nicoya
p.74

PROVINCIA
SAN JOSÉ

Golfo
de Nicoya

Playa Montezuma
16 Montezuma

Jacó

10 km
6.21 mi

MONTEVERDE

(□ E4) **Monteverde is an extensive range of cloud forests at a height of 1,300m to 1,800m, home to several government-owned and private nature reserves. You can visit them from the main town of Santa Elena (population 4,000) on an organised tour, by hire car or by bus.**

A dozen North American Quaker families came here in the 1950s and founded the farm and settlement of Monteverde. The 300-hectare cloud forest *Reserva Bosque Nuboso Santa Elena* is the responsibility of the group. It contains numerous trails, including paved hiking trails. The private *Monteverde Cloud Forest Biological Reserve*, maintained by the international research group Centro Científico Tropical *(cct.or.cr)*, is 6km east of Santa Elena (bus link). The reserve, which originally measured only 3km², now covers an area of 50km². The so-called Children's Rainforest (Bosque Eterno de los Niños) is maintained by a successful (private) conservation organisation and has numerous hiking trails *(senderos)*.

The tranquil town of *Santa Elena* is now a hotspot for visitors: shops and tour operators line the main street and there are organic restaurants as well as reiki and yoga practitioners. If you have travelled here from the lowlands via the steep winding road, you will notice that it is pleasantly cool in Monteverde, with average temperatures of around 18°C and frequent rain, so rainwear and waterproof hiking boots should be part of your outfit. You are on the cusp of weather zones here, so forecasting is difficult.

SIGHTSEEING

EL TRAPICHE

This old-fashioned sugar mill with a patio restaurant still produces sugar cane juice today. You'll see a lot on a two-hour tour of the farm, and things are explained in a really interesting and exciting way. Juan Hidalgo and his family also grow coffee beans here, then roast them and produce fabulous gourmet coffee. *¡Muy simpático!* You'll take an ox cart to the last stop on the tour, to see where fine chocolate is made from cocoa beans. *Tours daily 10am, 1pm, 3pm | 2km northwest of Santa Elena, pick-up in town available for a fee | tel. 60 17 20 20 | eltrapiche tour.com*

RESERVA BOSQUE NUBOSO SANTA ELENA (SANTA ELENA CLOUD FOREST RESERVE) ★ 🐾

Towering clouds above gigantic trees, mosses, epiphytes and lianas. Glistening drops of water on shining orchids, wafts of mist, gurgling streams and roaring waterfalls. The croaking, chattering and chirping of countless frogs and birds. It all adds up to an intense sensory experience! Despite the many visitors, the fabulously beautiful cloud forest has lost none of its magic. Local schoolchildren and Canadian helpers created the small, less crowded protected area with courses for biology students and

INSIDER TIP
Spot a rare bird

several kilometres of nature trails. Nowhere else are the chances so good that you will see a quetzal, a rare bird recognisable by its metre-long tail feathers. Guided hikes are also offered. *Daily 7am–4pm | 7km northeast of Santa Elena | reservasantaelena.org*

JARDÍN DE MARIPOSAS (MONTEVERDE BUTTERFLY GARDENS)

Scared of spiders? The turquoise and green specimens here may fascinate you so much that they cure your phobia. And of course, there are plenty of butterflies as well. The American founder is a taxonomist, so there are four strictly divided enclosures. It's fascinating to be in the rearing chamber – the nursery, if you like – and be fortunate enough to see a butterfly that has just emerged from its cocoon. *Daily 9am–3.30pm | turn right off the Santa Elena–Monteverde road | monteverdebutterflygardens.com | ⏱ 2–3 hrs*

BOSQUE ETERNO DE LOS NIÑOS (CHILDREN'S ETERNAL RAINFOREST) ⚑ 👥

A rainforest for children! Only in Costa Rica: children from 44 nations donated money to open the country's biggest, private nature reserve. Today, schools around the world continue to collect money to maintain the Bosque Eterno. The organisation is also always on the lookout for young volunteers (18 and over) to help run tourist groups or to work in the rainforest

(*engageglobally.org.*) The *Sendero Bajo de Tigre* (3.5km) is one of the trails that is signposted for hikers, and although there are hardly any feline predators, you may well encounter

Star of the Santa Elena Reserve: the quetzal, with its metre-long tail

Treetop trail: the Skywalk in the Santa Elena Reserve

monkeys, toucans and coati – and perhaps even the occasional sloth. Of course, there is also a child-friendly visitor centre and a children's educational trail. *Daily 8am–4.30pm | 3km southeast of Santa Elena | acmcr.org*

RESERVA BIOLÓGICA BOSQUE NUBOSO MONTEVERDE

In this nature reserve, the protection of the uniquely beautiful cloud forest is taken seriously: in order to preserve the delicate balance, only a maximum of 160 people are allowed in at any one time. During the season, the park entrance is sometimes closed to additional visitors as early as the morning. So make sure that you are at the entrance shortly before it opens! You can go on your own, but the tours with local guides are a special experience. *Daily 7am–4pm | 6km southeast of Santa Elena | cloudforestmonteverde. com*

INSIDER TIP
The early bird
...

EATING & DRINKING

ORCHID COFFEE SHOP

Cosy venue with (organic) cuisine: varied bowls and vegetarian dishes, and the home-made lemonades and various types of coffee are great. If the fog is particularly thick (again), the cocoa with orange and ginger will warm you up! *Santa Elena | Ctra. 620 at junction with Ctra. 606 | tel. 26 45 68 50 | orchidcoffeecr.com | $$*

SABOR TICO

The *casado* – rice, beans, fried plantain and warm tortillas – is delicious, as are the other plain dishes that are served here. Lovely view of the town from the terrace. *Santa Elena | Ctra. 620 (opposite the Megasuper) | tel. 26 45 59 68 | restaurantesabortico.com | $$*

TAQUERÍA TACO TACO

What is the secret of these delicious tacos? We don't know but you'd better try one quickly! *Santa Elena | Ctra. 606 (diagonally opposite the Supercompro) | tacotaco.net | $*

SHOPPING

CASEM

The Women's Cooperative souvenir shop sells hand-made wooden toys, small wall carpets, eco T-shirts and excellent Monteverde coffee. *Santa Elena–Monteverde road, 300m before the cheese factory | casemcoop. blogspot.com*

HELADERÍA Y FÁBRICA DE QUESOS MONTEVERDE

The legendary Quaker cheese factory, now owned by a Mexican corporation (*Sigma-alimentos.com*), produces over a dozen types of cheese that are sold all over the country. Here you can shop at the source – be sure to try the creamy chocolate ice-cream

IDER TIP
Chocolate ice-cream, please!

with candied fruit! *Santa Elena–Monteverde road, 300m southeast of Casem*

SPORT & ACTIVITIES

SABINE'S SMILING HORSES 😀

Various stables provide horses so you can explore the area on horseback. Sabine's is a reliable operator, with well-groomed horses and various tours, including the *Campesino Tour* (🕐 *2 hrs*) on mountain trails with great views. Booking required. *2km west of Santa Elena | tel. 83 85 24 24 | horseback-riding-tour.com*

SELVATURA ADVENTURE PARK

In this private cloud forest, hanging bridges take you through the treetops, and there is a butterfly and humming-bird garden and an insect museum. You will also see numerous sloths, which are reared back to strength here. Many enjoy the thrill of the *Canopy Tour*, which consists of 15 zip lines that take you 3km into the cloud forest. *Daily 8.30am–4pm, booking required | 7km north-east of Santa Elena | selvatura.com*

SKYWALK ⭐

Wow! Six hanging bridges combine in a 500m-long path through the 40m-high treetops of the cloud forest! The guided 😀 *Treetop Walk* is a perfectly safe adventure for children, too. You have a choice between zip lines and suspension bridge hikes at canopy level, and a comfortable journey through the cloud forest in the *Sky Tram. Guided tours almost hourly until*

A paradise for water lovers: the Tabacón thermal spa – one of many around La Fortuna

3pm | 3.5km in the direction of the Santa Elena Reserve | skyadventures. travel

LAGUNA DE ARENAL

(◫ D–E3) **The 40km-long reservoir is one of the best inland surfing spots in the world.**

Constant trade winds (at their strongest between January and April) come courtesy of the funnel-like, 1,633m-high ★ *Arenal Volcano* east of the lake. The view of the active volcano from the southwest bank or the Parqueo Interior (3km to the west) is fabulous in good weather, when you can see the perfect cone shape of the volcano against the clear sky. The windsurfing, kitesurfing and SUP centre *Tico Windsurf (ticowind.com)* on the western shore has been the place to go for surfers for over two decades; here you will find excellent equipment for kitesurfing. There are also nice cafés and restaurants run by expats on the western shore, as well as cute cottages and guesthouses for overnight stays.

DESTINATIONS ON LAKE ARENAL

1 THERMAL POOLS AROUND LA FORTUNA ★

In La Fortuna and the surrounding area are several thermal pools: the Arenal Volcano provides water at a temperature between 25°C and 45°C, with healing minerals, and the spring is constantly replenishing the pools with new water.

The *Balneario Tabacón*, 12km west of La Fortuna, belongs to the luxury hotel *Tabacón Grand Spa Thermal Resort (tabacon.com)* and is the best, albeit pricy, hot spring for wellness and relaxation. Rainforest vegetation and a dozen pools styled with huge rocks are the key feature of the *Baldi Hot Springs (baldihotsprings.cr)* at the resort of the same name, 4km west of La Fortuna, which are much more reasonably priced. The *Eco Termales La Fortuna (ecotermalesfortuna.cr)* opposite has five pools.

The *Springs Resort & Spa (the springscostarica.com)* is situated on a huge tropical estate 13km northwest of La Fortuna. The main building, with large, luxurious rooms and suites, is surrounded by numerous hot springs, thermal pools and chlorinated pools, some with spectacular views of the volcano, and one of the best spas in the country. Day visitors are also welcome. *You can relax in four pools at a particularly reasonable price at the* 🐗 *Termales Laureles (termaleslaureles. com).* The spas are located 7km west of La Fortuna and admission is just 5,000 colones (approx. $10).

INSIDER TIP
Bargain relaxation!

② MISTICO PARK

Up for some thrills? Then get yourself to Mistico's *Puentes Colgantes*, a 3km-long trail that can be quite a challenge because it is frequently interrupted by hanging bridges up to 100m long, including several that look quite scary!

INSIDER TIP
For thrill seekers

The trail has fantastic views of the Arenal Volcano and the Cordillera Central. You can also go on exciting excursions on horseback. *Daily 6am–4.30pm | 4km west of Tabacón, turning at the reservoir, then 2km on a well-made road | misticopark.com*

③ ARENAL NATURA ECOLOGICAL PARK

This nature reserve is on the road between La Fortuna and the volcano, 300m northeast of the Volcano Lodge hotel. There's a two-hour guided tour with lots of information on around 25 frog and toad species, all in lovely terrariums, and also a number of snakes and crocodiles. *Daily 8.30am–4.30pm | arenalnatura.com*

④ BUTTERFLY CONSERVATORY 🏞 👥

The Butterfly Conservatory is located to the south of the lake with views of both the lake and the volcano. Tropical butterflies flutter about the butterfly house, next door frogs croak, and you'll smell the medicinal herbs on a walk through the rainforest. *Daily 10am–4pm | down gravel track near southeast corner of Avenal Lake | butterflyconservatory.org*

⑤ ECOCENTRO DANAUS

Around 2.5km east of La Fortuna (towards San Carlos) is this private, multiple-award-winning conservation area run by enthusiastic staff. The 90-minute tours offer the opportunity to meet Maleku people, members of a small indigenous tribe. Based some 50km from La Fortuna, they live by agriculture and fishing, and come here to sell their hand-made bows and arrows and balsa wood sculptures. It' one of the rare opportunities to meet the Malekus, who speak Spanish alongside the Maleku language. *Daily 8am–5pm, booking required | eco centrodanaus.com*

INSIDER TIP
Chat with the Malekus

LIBERIA

(☐ C3) **During the summer, heat and dust cover the light-coloured, tufa-plastered roads and white houses, which gave Liberia the name "Ciudad Blanca" – white town.**

The capital (population 67,000) of the province of Guanacaste was built on the banks of the Río Liberia in a chequerboard pattern. It's a rather placid town, a shopping and entertainment destination at weekends for the *sabaneros* working on the cattle and horse farms in the region. Liberia's location on the Carretera Interamericana, as the Pan-American Highway is called in Costa Rica, brings through traffic to the town, and also makes it a starting point for visits to the Nicoya Peninsula, with its popular beaches, and to the Santa Rosa and Rincón de la Vieja national parks.

Horses are broken in on the many ranches in the region around Liberia and competitions are held for entertainment, with men riding wild bulls. On 25 July, the *Día de Guanacaste*, you can experience cattle shows and rodeos everywhere. In the first week of September, rodeos take place during the *Semana Cultural*.

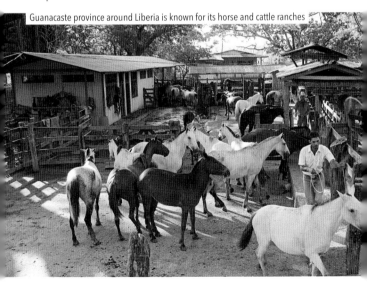
Guanacaste province around Liberia is known for its horse and cattle ranches

SIGHTSEEING

SUN DOORS 🚩

Many of the local houses have the *puerta del sol* that is typical of the town: two outside doors lead into the houses from the northeast and northwest. In bygone days, the door facing the sun was left open so light could come in; today, with electricity, residents leave the door facing away from the sun open to let fresh air in while keeping the heat out.

EATING & DRINKING

EL BRAMADERO

People at El Bramadero have been preparing juicy steaks for over 50 years. Locals and visitors sit at long tables to enjoy the barbecued meals. Vegetarians are happy with the generous salads. *Panamericana/Av. 1 (next*

to McDonald's) | tel. 26 66 03 71 | hotelbramadero.com | $$

EL CAFÉ LIBERIA

Set in the *Casa Zuñiga*, a wonderfully atmospheric colonial house, this place not only serves the best *Tico* cuisine, but also international classics such as caesar salad and pasta. Rich desserts, cakes and speciality coffees round off the menu. Excellent on every level. *C/ Real | tel. 26 65 16 60 | $*

AROUND LIBERIA

6 PONDEROSA ADVENTURE PARK

10km south of Liberia / 15 mins on the Ctra. Interamericana

This private animal reserve is home to elephants, giraffes and zebras, and you can enjoy spotting them on a wildlife tour with a ranger. Another fabulous experience is riding on the beautifully-cared-for horses. *Daily 9am–5pm | ponderosacostarica.com | ▥ C3*

7 PARQUE NACIONAL RINCÓN DE LA VIEJA ⭐

25km northeast of Liberia / 45 mins via Curubandé

The magnificent national park with a wide variety of vegetation zones surrounds two volcanoes: the Rincón de la Vieja (1,895m) and Santa María (1,916m). Hot sulphur springs, fumaroles and crater lakes characterise the geothermally active, tropical jungle area, which is home to more than 250 bird species. It's an extremely water-rich treasure trove: over 30 streams and rivers have their source in the park and nurture the almost impenetrable greenery. Guides are available at the "Las Pailas" entrance. *Tue–Sun 8am–3pm | ⊞ C2*

🟦 BEACHES

There are countless developed beaches some 30km west of Liberia on the *Papagayo Peninsula,* where you find around 30 tiny beaches and bays along the 25km-long coast, backed by cliffs. South of the Papagayo Peninsula, the *Playa Hermosa,* with sparkling blue water that gently laps the bay with soft ways, lives up to its name of "Lovely Beach". *⊞ B3*

PENÍNSULA DE NICOYA

(⊞ A–D 4–6) **The darker skin of many residents here is testimony to the ancestors of the cattle breeders who settled on the peninsula: the indigenous Chorotega people.**

They also gave the peninsula its name, "Land surrounded by water on both sides", because it stretches about 100km into the ocean. There are numerous attractive beaches, some of them sleepy and remote, others more lively, all around the peninsula.

Take plenty of time to find your way around here, because not many of the roads are tarmacked, and travelling on them is quite an adventure. However, the beach that is served by only one bus a day is often the loveliest. You'll find all levels of accommodation around the beaches, from a hot-and-humid boarding house room in the centre of a beachside town to an air-conditioned bungalow with ocean views.

DESTINATIONS ON NICOYA

🟦 NICOYA

This small town (population 25,000) in the middle of the peninsula is the cultural centre and a perfect stop-off on the way to the coast. Built on the foundation walls of an old indigenous settlement by the Spanish in 1544, it is home to the country's second-oldest church. The *Iglesia de San Blas* (called after the town's old name) was built in 1634 on the site where the vanquished *indígenas* held their religious rituals. This place of worship, white with red tiles and an impressive bell tower, is opposite the town's mango tree-shaded *Parque Central.* *⊞ B–C4*

🟦 GUAITIL

The tiny town of Guaitil is known as the centre of ceramics production. Many hotels decorate their foyers with the bulbous vases in the pre-Columbian style. The vases, jugs and pots are fired in clay-walled kilns by indigenous families. *⊞ B4*

11 SANTA CRUZ

This small town (population 22,000) is the country's self-styled "folklore capital". The music tradition, which is practised all year round, has its highlight in mid-January, when traditional dances are performed and costumed dancers process through the town. Local specialities are served at the *sodas* around the municipal park. □ *B4*

12 TAMARINDO

Whether surfing, partying or relaxing on a beach, you can do it all – and more – in Tamarindo (population 6,500). As one of the hottest spots in the entire region, it also has some outstanding restaurants, exceptional boutiques and Spanish language schools. By day, the propeller aircraft from San José land at the tiny airport, but there are still plenty of opportunities for finding peaceful bliss – for example just to the north on ✱ *Playa Grande*. The beautiful, unspoilt beach not only delights swimmers, but also wildlife conservationists: from November to March, turtles come here on moonlit nights to lay their eggs. Also dreamlike, half an hour's drive further north, is ✱ *Playa Conchal*: crystal-clear water, no currents and excellent for snorkelling. The golden-yellow, sandy beach consists – as the name suggests – of small crushed shells (Spanish: *concha*). □ *A4*

The call of the board – or the nearest beach bar: Tamarindo is the region's holiday hub

Steady drops of water form stalactites in the Terciopelo cave in Barra Honda

13 PARQUE NACIONAL BARRA HONDA

An experience for cave visitors and bat fans: this park, 20km northeast of Nicoya, consists of a vast network of karst caves, 19 explored stalactite caves inhabited by colonies of bats, and many other caves that have not yet been explored. Streams flow through the caves, and there are some waterfalls between one cave and the next. Currently, only one cave – Terciopelo – is open to visitors.

To visit the caves, you must have the required equipment, experience and support. The park management offers tours, but you must book in advance. It is also worth walking along the signposted *Sendero Ceiba* to a *lookout point* with views over the tropical forest and the Nicoya Peninsula. *Park daily 8am–4pm | tel. 26 59 15 51 | nicoyapeninsula.com/barrahonda | C4*

14 PARQUE NACIONAL PALO VERDE

This wetland at the mouth of the Río Tempisque on the Gulf of Nicoya is a green jewel in Costa Rica's driest province. Mangrove forests and swamps, lagoons and low, evergreen forest areas form a unique habitat and are home to many rare water birds. The boat tours lasting several hours (*paloverdeboattours.com*) on the Río Tempisque – the river with the most crocodiles in the entire country – are great. *Daily 8am–5pm | C3–4*

15 SÁMARA

A key destination for many European visitors and *Ticos* alike is the palm-studded ✹ *Playa Sámara* in the west of the peninsula. The gently rounded bay, bordered by the Punto Indio cliff, has one of the safest and quietest beaches in Costa Rica, with clear water, excellent food and a gentle atmosphere. Sámara is *pura vida*, but please be aware that it can get pretty busy here, especially at weekends, because wealthy *Ticos* have their summer homes in Sámara. ▢ *B5*

16 MONTEZUMA

Start the day by saluting the sun and enjoy the evening under a fabulous starry sky with a cocktail in the beach bar – live and let live is the motto in the fishing village of Montezuma in the extreme south, where lots of escapists and ageing hippies join the *Ticos*. The lovely, unspoilt ✹ sandy beach is surrounded by cliffs, the jungle reaches almost as far as the water – where you should watch out for dangerous currents – and the cafés, small restaurants and hotels, some quite improvised, are trendy meeting places. There is even a *Farmer's Market (Sat 9am–1pm | Parque Principal)* with organically grown fruit and vegetables, and wholefood cakes. The secluded, rock-framed *Playa Cocalito*, 10km to the northeast, presents itself in picture-perfect colours. Can you spot the beautiful *waterfall* that pours into the sea at the northern end of the bay? ▢ *D6*

INSIDER TIP
Wonders of nature included

LUXURY WITH DREAMY VIEWS

You'll find a spectacular holiday spot at the *Lagarta Lodge (Nosara | tel. 40 70 11 44 | lagartalodge.com | $$$)*, which is under Swiss management. With just 26 suites, stylish luxury and breath-taking views are perfectly combined. You can experience the lushness of nature in its own reserve, while regular shuttle buses take you to the best beach and surf spots in Nosara.

CAMPING, BUT NOT AS WE KNOW IT

A stay at the *Chira Glamping Monteverde (Cerro Plano Sapo Dorado Road | tel. 84 56 10 22 | chiraglamping.com | $$$)* in Santa Elena is a very different kind of camping experience. You stay on a terrace in a mega-chic sleeping tent with large windows, a yoga mat, Bose speakers and a private hot tub. You'll also have a great bathroom and an outdoor shower with a view of the rainforest. Camping on another level!

PACIFIC COAST

DARK SAND AND GREEN PALMS

Between Puntarenas and the Corcovado National Park lie long stretches of sea backed by verdant nature. The proximity to the central plateau – less than two hours' drive and with an hourly bus service – makes the coast particularly attractive for people in the capital, although it is the southern, more distant coast that is really exciting.

Manuel Antonio, Costa Rica's best-known national park and a little gem, is also located here. The park is busy, especially at weekends

A day trip in a catamaran from Puntarenas to the snorkelling paradise off the Isla Tortuga

and during high season. Too much hustle and bustle for your taste? More remote and still largely unspoilt is the southern Pacific coast, with the Osa Peninsula. Once prosperous thanks to banana cultivation, the region has put its trust in eco-tourism following the demise of this monoculture. There are great eco-lodges and nature reserves in some spectacular locations. The Corcovado National Park is part of the largest contiguous rainforest in Central America: go on a tour here to experience this up close.

PACIFIC COAST

PROVINCIA
HEREDIA

PROVINCIA
ALAJUELA

Espíritu
Santo

Puntarenas
p. 82

1

San Mateo

Orotina

Atenas

Alajuela

27

3

San Pablo

San José

Ciudad Colón

Heredia

32

2

**San
José**

Tres
Ríos

23

34

Parque Nacional Carara 1

*Golfo
de Nicoya*

135km, 2¾ hrs

PROVINCIA SAN JOSÉ

315km, 4¾ hrs

Jacó

34

Parrita

Isla Damas 2

Quepos
p. 84

3

**Parque Nacional
Manuel Antonio** ★

Espadilla Sur,
Manuel Antonio,
Playa Escondida

*OCÉANO
PACÍFICO*

60km, 1 hr

MARCO POLO HIGHLIGHTS

★ **PARQUE NACIONAL MANUEL ANTONIO**
The smallest national park is also the most
beautiful: picture perfect. ➤ p. 85

★ **BAHÍA DRAKE**
This palm-fringed cove is one of Costa
Rica's most remote places. ➤ p. 88

★ **PARQUE NACIONAL CORCOVADO**
The "Amazon of Costa Rica". ➤ p. 89

20 km
12.43 mi

PUNTARENAS

(🗺 E5) **A traditional resort for *Ticos*, and the capital (population 120,000) of the province of the same name, Puntarenas was the country's main Pacific harbour until the development of Puerto Caldera in the south.**

Puntarenas, which grew from the coffee trade, covers a 6km-long headland in the Gulf of Nicoya. The humid subtropical climate is ideal for growing the rice, bananas and coconut palms for which Puntarenas is still a trading centre.

On the south side of the city is a long stretch of beach where locals have their second homes – this is where the boats are. Idyllic? Not really. It's a busy area, which at times seems to drown in rubbish.

A stroll along the beach promenade *Paseo de los Turistas* (on the south side) will take you past pleasant restaurants, cafés and bars; on the north side of the city, you'll pass the harbour basin, with docks, warehouses and ferry terminals – the working quarters of a port city. The streets of the city centre *(Calles 1–7)* and the *market (Mercado Municipal) (Av. 3/C/ 2)* bustle with life in the mornings.

SIGHTSEEING

PARQUE MARINO DEL PACÍFICO
👥🎋

Education made interesting, especially for children: attractions include the crocodile-breeding basins, turtles

The subtropical climate of Puntarenas turns a balcony into a greenhouse

and tropical fish in this beautifully designed state park that is committed to protecting the ocean. *Tue–Sun 9am–4.30pm | Av. 4, old railway station, 500m east of the cruise ship pier | parquemarino.org | ◷ 1½ hrs*

EATING & DRINKING

CAPITÁN MORENO

Juicy steaks, generous plates of seafood and a large selection of craft beers. And parties: DJs, bands, dancing and general merry-making. *Paseo de los Turistas/C/ 13–15 | tel. 26 61 08 10 | $$*

SHOPPING

The sweetest mangos, mini bananas by the dozen and *pan dulce* (sweet bread) are well-priced at the *Mercado Municipal (Av. 3/C/ 2)*.

SPORT & ACTIVITIES

TORTUGA ISLAND CRUISE

A catamaran takes you to uninhabited Tortuga Island for snorkelling in the crystal-clear water, white beaches, nature and buffets on the sand. Organised by *Bay Island Cruises (tel. 22 35 35 36 | bayislandcruises.com)*.

NIGHTLIFE

The cool evening is the best time to visit one of the bars or nice restaurants on the Paseo de los Turistas; watching the sun set over the mountains of Nicoya is a sight you'll never forget.

AROUND PUNTARENAS

◨ PARQUE NACIONAL CARARA
50km southeast of Puntarenas / 1 hr on the N34

Bordered on the north by the Río Tárcoles, this national park has a tremendous level of biodiversity thanks to its different vegetation zones. For example, it's home to one of the largest macaw colonies in the country, of the rare scarlet macaw. With red heads, chests and wing tips, and blue and yellow wings, these birds are over 80cm long, and announce their presence with a penetrating call. They leave the park at sunrise and sunset to fly to the mangroves on the coast. You're most likely to see them with a local guide, for example from *Vic Tours (tel. 87 23 30 08 | victourscostarica. com)*. Following the Carara trails with Victor

INSIDER TIP
Insider knowledge

is both fun and hugely informative. There are two trails on the west side of the park, one of which runs 500m south of the bridge over the Río Tárcoles, where you will usually see crocodiles on the river bank. *Daily May–Nov 8am–4pm, Dec–April 7am–4pm | booking in advance required at sinac.go.cr | ▥ F6*

QUEPOS

(□ G7) **Beaches, lodges and rainforest: Quepos (population 20,000) is the gateway to Manuel Antonio, Costa Rica's best-known national park, a few miles away. The town retains its flair from the days when it was a busy banana port.**

Puerto Quepos was built as a harbour for export, but after the banana plantations were destroyed by an epidemic in the 1950s, things started to go downhill. The unexciting drive to Quepos leads through oil palm plantations, but as you approach, you'll notice the little town's pretty location among hilly forests. It may have been this that led the Franciscans to build a mission station on the Naranjo River in 1570, although they abandoned it in 1730.

Only a few foundation walls are left of the station. Today, Quepos consists of *Boca Vieja*, an old village of pile dwellings near the bridge over the funnel-shaped estuary, the bungalows of the former banana growers outside the town, and the relatively new centre.

EATING & DRINKING

EL PATIO DE CAFÉ MILAGRO

Iconic meeting place for young Americans. This coffee roastery, which was established by a college student, offers speciality coffees, while the colourful open-air restaurant serves Costa Rican dishes and international cuisine, including fish, from breakfast until dinner, as well as cocktails and South American wines. They often have live music too. *On the road to Manuel Antonio, km 4 | tel. 27 77 22 72 | elpatiodecafemilagro.com | $$*

RUNAWAY GRILL RESTAURANT & FISH BAR

Happy hour, sunsets and a "you hook them, we cook them" offer for anglers. Dinner followed by a visit to the 🐖 *Outdoor Movie Nights* is an excellent combination. *Marina Pez Vela/Paseo del Mar | tel. 25 19 90 95 | runaway-grill.com | $$–$$$*

SPORT & ACTIVITIES

AMIGOS DEL RÍO

Boat trips out onto the ocean, as well as white-water rafting, horse-riding and jungle hikes. *On the road to Manuel Antonio, km 2 | tel. 27 77 00 82 | amigosdelrio.net*

AROUND QUEPOS

🄻 ISLA DAMAS

5km northwest of Quepos / by boat from Quepos Marina

The elongated peninsula near Quepos forms a lagoon into which four rivers flow. There are dense mangroves around the mouth of the lagoon, which is also home to lots of water fowl. *□ G7*

The Manuel Antonio National Park is a great place to spot monkeys

🔳 PARQUE NACIONAL MANUEL ANTONIO ★ ☂

7km south of Quepos / 15 mins on the Ctra. 618

The three bays of the national park are considered the loveliest in the country; two of them, the white beach bays ☂ *Espadilla Sur* and ☂ *Manuel Antonio*, are separated by the impressive rock formation *Punta Catedral*. The vegetation, which almost reaches the water's edge, and the little monkeys looking for leftovers, create a tropical atmosphere. The park is home to lots of lizards, water fowl, raccoons and 200 bird species. At its southeastern edge, off the beaten track, is the fabulous ☂ *Playa Escondida*, which is much quieter. The park also has 12 small islands that you can see from the shore – they're breeding grounds for sea birds.

Useful for visitors with children who can't walk very far yet but still want to see the monkeys: the park has several short, circular trails and, if you like, you can be back at the starting point in a couple of hours. The biodiversity on these is no less than anywhere else in the park, and contact with monkeys is guaranteed.

The national park is well visited all year round. As you approach the park, con artists use whistles and jump out in front of cars in a threatening manner, trying to make drivers use their overpriced parking facilities – just keep driving. *Wed–Mon 7am–4pm | booking in advance required at sinac. go.cr | manuelantoniopark.com | 🔲 G7*

UVITA

(🔲 J8) **In a great strategic location for experiencing the southern Pacific, the friendly town of Uvita (population 5,000) sits beside the shimmering waters of the ocean.**

Uvita is *the* place for whale-watching

The coast around Uvita is known as *Costa Ballena*, the "Whale Coast", and is considered the centre for whale-watching tours par excellence. Here you can experience the marine giants in their natural habitat every year between the end of July and mid-November, and between the end of December and mid-April – an unforgettable experience! Incidentally, from the air, the headland off Uvita, part of the Ballena National Park, looks like a whale's fin.

INSIDER TIP
On the whale's fin

A marvellous coincidence! At low tide, you can walk around the bay on the headland and go swimming and snorkelling there. The vegetation in this little paradise is dark green and lush, and many streams, small rivers and waterfalls are just waiting to be discovered.

SIGHTSEEING

PARQUE NACIONAL MARINO BALLENA

The entire coast south of the village is part of the national park. Its dark sandy beach offers great opportunities for swimming, snorkelling and surfing. The park is teeming with animals: dolphins, turtles, schools of fish, an immense variety of birds – and of course whales, which you might even see from the beach if you're lucky. Many paths at the various park entrances invite you to explore nature within. Three areas of the national park are open to visitors, and tickets are valid all day for all parts of the park. *Sector Uvita and Colonia daily 7am–6pm, Sector Ballena daily 8am–6pm | booking in advance required at sinac.go.cr*

EATING & DRINKING

TRIBU

A meeting place for young and old. Healthy and delicious international cuisine with a slight Asian flavour. *Calle Bejuco, 200m south of the Uvita waterfall | tel. 89 89 24 86 | $–$$*

VILLAS ALTURAS

In a hotel at the Alturas Wildlife Sanctuary, you will find this unusual restaurant serving fresh fish and meat as well as delicious pasta dishes. A breath-taking view over the coast is guaranteed. *Tel. 22 00 54 40 | villasalturas.com | $$*

SHOPPING

FARMERS' MARKET

Farmers, mostly expats from all over the area, offer their products and specialities at the market – fresh and organically grown. *Wed, Sat 8am–2pm | main road near the Bahia Ballena supermarket*

SPORT & ACTIVITIES

There are few more exciting experiences than following a whale with a calf in their natural environment. Tours are offered during the whale-watching months mentioned above. *Bahia Adventures (tel. 27 43 83 62 | bahiaaventuras.com)* have made a name for themselves as a responsible tour operator: the boats keep a respectful distance from the animals so as not to disturb them in their habitat. The *Uvita waterfall (access daily, in daylight | Barrio los Ángeles, next to the entrance to Cascada Verde Lodge)* is not particularly high, nor does it move huge amounts of water, but it is beautiful, easy to reach on foot and charges only a small admission fee. Here you can experience how the *Ticos* like to spend their leisure time: playing in the water, jumping off the rocks … It's a bit like being in a lively swimming pool. There is a simple but good restaurant right at the entrance – ideal for refreshments.

BEACHES

The beaches in the national park are protected. You pay a park admission fee of $6.80 and can visit them from 7am to 6pm that day. But there are also plenty of beautiful stretches outside the park, for example, ⚲ *Playa Ventanas* (Window Beach): at low tide, entrances to various caves open up on the beach; when the water returns, they are flooded. *Playa Tortuga*, a turtle sanctuary, is a real gem. Between June and December, you can witness the laying of eggs here and later see the baby turtles hatch. The *Reserva Playa Tortuga (reservaplayatortuga. org)* is responsible for the sanctuary's management. The *playa* is also suitable for swimming, but as with almost all Pacific beaches: beware of the strong currents!

AROUND UVITA

⁴ ALTURAS WILDLIFE SANCTUARY

13km northwest of Uvita / 15 mins on the N34

The sanctuary is located near San Martín Norte between Uvita and Dominical. It rehabilitates injured animals that cannot survive on their own and releases them back into the wild if possible. Otherwise, they find a new home here. *Tue–Sun, tours at 9am, 11am, 1pm, booking required | tel. 86 09 53 63 | alturaswildlifesanctuary. org | ⌖ H8*

Dense forest provides a home for many species: Parque Nacional Corcovado

PENÍNSULA DE OSA

(ஶ J–K 9–10) **Lush rainforest, count-less waterfalls and a huge variety of wildlife: the Osa Peninsula is an absolute highlight of the Pacific coast.**

It can be reached quite quickly from Uvita. If you are travelling from the central plateau, you can take Ruta 2 (journey time around seven hours) through Costa Rica's diverse land-scapes: first, the road winds its way up the country's highest pass, the 3491m *Cerro de la Muerte*, which is usually shrouded in fog, then it takes you along tight bends into the *Valle del General*. Green pineapple fields stretch for miles across the red earth. In places, the road follows the course of rivers and passes waterfalls. From

Palmar Norte it gets humid, the vege-tation tropical, with orchids, bananas and palm trees.

DESTINATIONS ON THE PENINSULA

⑤ BAHÍA DRAKE ★

On the peninsula's northwest side is the *Bahía Drake*, a largely undevel-oped natural paradise with clean beaches and dense vegetation – a wonderful habitat for countless wild animals. Excursions and tours are offered on foot, on horseback or by boat – great for nature lovers and adventurous travellers. The accommo-dation providers are happy to help with the organisation of your trips. There are several options for travelling to Bahía Drake. *Sansa Airlines* fly directly from San José. A more excit-ing option is to travel by bus, hire car or taxi to the town of Sierpe *(ஶ K9)* and from there take a *lancha*, a boat that travels down the Río Sierpe to the bay in just under 1½ hours. Drake Bay is now also easily accessible by off-road vehicle. The route leads from Chacarita via the RN245 to Rincón and from there on a dirt road (approx. 1½ hours' drive). *J9–10*

⑥ PARQUE NACIONAL CORCOVADO ★

In the 1960s the sparsely populated peninsula was still one huge greenhouse, but by 1975 a considerable proportion of the precious woods had fallen victim to over-exploitation – until the 420km² national park was created in the peninsula's southwest. Gold was later discovered in the park's rivers. Adventurers tried their luck, a real gold rush set in and the destruction of the nature reserve continued. Today, mining is prohibited in the national park, which Costa Ricans call "our Amazon". Dense greenery provides a home for numerous animals, and even big wild cats pay their respects – seeing them is an exciting, and mostly harmless, experience. The park has six entrances, and Sector San Pedrillo and Sector Los Planes can be reached via Drake Bay. *Daily 7am–4pm | booking in advance required at reservacionespnc@sinac.go.cr or tel. 27 35 50 36 | J–K10*

EATING & DRINKING

RESTAURANTE LOOKOUT 🐷

An insider tip for eating cheaply in this area. Don Michael doesn't offer anything fancy, but he serves inventive cuisine with fresh ingredients. *Bahía Drake | northeastern part of the beach near the Mirador Lodge hotel | tel. 88 36 94 15 | $*

SPORT & ACTIVITIES

BOAT TOUR TO THE ISLA DEL CAÑO

The small Isla del Caño (*H9–10*) off the coast is part of the Corcovado National Park. Boat tours in small groups are offered in Drake – the trip takes less than an hour from there. Once on the island, you can discover a crystal-clear underwater paradise by snorkelling or diving. We recommend that you book the tour several weeks in advance. Contact your accommodation for assistance. Alternatively, the *Corcovado Info Centre (Agujitas | main road, next to the Allegra Hostel | tel. 88 46 47 34 | corcovadoinfocenter. com)* has proven to be a good option.

BEACHES

There are fantastic beaches along the Bahía Drake, the local *Playa Colorada* just being the first one.

INSIDER TIP
Hike from beach to beach

A hiking trail runs parallel to the coastline from beach to beach as far as Los Planes, where the Corcovado National Park begins. After crossing the Río Agujitas on a daring (!) suspension bridge, the trail heads west. Monkeys and sloths are omnipresent; the sounds from the jungle can be frightening, but don't worry – most of the animals sound bigger than they actually are.

The most beautiful beaches, which are also suitable for swimming, can be found in Bahía Las Caletas. Crystal-clear water, coral and pure nature await you at the ✳ Playa Las Caletas. But as everywhere in this part of the world, beware of the strong currents of the surging Pacific.

GOLFITO

(∏ L10) **Golfito (population 12,000) stretches over 6km along a lagoon of the Golfo Dulce.**

Half a century ago, the port was the top exporter of bananas; 20,000 people settled in the area, and bars and brothels opened in the old town. It's quieter today. A new free-trade zone (depósito, for tax-free shopping) and the development of tourism are intended to bring in visitors and create jobs.

Pueblo Cívico is the oldest part of Golfito, and is in the south of the town. You'll find hotels, restaurants and bars here, as well as a small dock (muellecito) for boats and water taxis for rides to the beaches. The modern town centre starts on the northern edge of Pueblo Cívico, around the Centro Turístico Samoa Sur. Further north is the wealthy Zona Americana.

EATING & DRINKING

MAR Y LUNA

Enjoy the sunset, the small harbour and the open ocean from the terrace with a beer in your hand – and afterwards, how about a tomato salad and guacamole? Or perhaps ceviche and a mariscada (with fish and crustaceans: excellent!). It gets busy at happy hour and when the regular live music is on. Ctra. 14/ km 3 | tel. 27 75 01 92 | $$

BEACHES

PLAYA CACAO

The dark gravel and sand beach is surrounded by dense rainforest – it's pure Robinson Crusoe. You can reach the playa by water taxi from the dock in Golfito (muellecito).

NIGHTLIFE

BAR LA BOMBA

It's the bomb! This place has been the meeting place for adventurers, lonely travellers, individualists and groups

An aromatic, invigorating delight: fresh ceviche

since 1946. Old photos on the walls of the restored bar trace Golfito's history. *Ctra. 14/ Pueblo Civil next to the service station*

AROUND GOLFITO

7 REFUGIO NACIONAL DE VIDA SILVESTRE GOLFITO
5km northwest of Golfito / 10 mins on the N14

Camping is permitted in the freely accessible animal reserve and tropical rainforest just outside the town. The best time to visit is between January and March when it is relatively dry. You will see lots of orchid and bird varieties in the park. *L9–10*

8 PARQUE INTERNACIONAL LA AMISTAD
100km to Las Tablas northeast of Golfito / 2½ hrs via Ciudad Neily

Costa Rica's biggest nature reserve crosses the border into Panama (1,900km² is on Costa Rican territory); it is also the least visited. It's mainly wilderness, largely without roads and with just a few trails to explore in the company of a local guide. The biodiversity here – deciduous and pine forests, tropical rainforest and moors, wasteland covered in low shrubs and grasses – surpasses all other national parks. There are 400 species of bird here, along with over 250 amphibians and reptiles, plus tapirs, jaguars, pumas, ocelots and several species of monkey.

WHERE TO STAY ON THE PACIFIC COAST

SUNSET CINEMA
Las Caletas Lodge (7 rooms | Playa Las Caletas | tel. 88 26 14 60 | caletaslodgedrake.com | $$) is beautifully located on the Bahía Drake and surrounded by pure nature. Away from the hustle and bustle, you can see the entire coast from a hill, experience the most beautiful sunsets, enjoy wonderful food and go on exciting tours.

AN EAGLE'S VIEW
La Mariposa (56 rooms and suites | tel. 27 77 03 55 | hotelmariposa. com | $$$), 4km south of Quepos, is one of the prettiest establishments in the region, high above the sea, furnished with antiques and ethnic objects. The furniture on the restaurant terrace glows in pink and turquoise.

Access on your own is extremely difficult. The starting point for adventurous hiking is the Altamira ranger station near the small village of the same name, which can only be reached by four-wheel drive. AsoProLA *(asoprola.com)*, a non-profit organisation which runs a café-restaurant there, arranges accommodation in guesthouses

> **INSIDER TIP**
> **Hands-on helpers**

and provides experienced guides for multi-day hikes through the rainforest. *K–M 7–8*

CARIBBEAN COAST

REGGAE, MANGROVES AND A LAID-BACK LIFE

The Atlantic coast is all about the Caribbean lifestyle: reggae music in the beach bars; tropical vegetation; brightly coloured wooden houses on stilts; fishing canoes under the palm trees, and the smell of the ocean and coconut in the air. Then there are the canals of Tortuguero surrounded by lush vegetation, and deserted sands with pelicans and frigate birds. And, on the humid Caribbean coast, many locals speak English in a variant of Jamaican patois.

In water, on land, in the air: Tortuguero National Park is practically one big zoo

While 98 per cent of the population in the rest of Costa Rica are descendants of European colonisers, one-third of the population in Limón province, bordering the Caribbean, are descendants of African slaves who were brought from the West Indies to work in the plantations and build the railway. Not only is the language different here, but so too is the lifestyle – music, food and the way of life are undeniably Caribbean. The province is sparsely populated: there are only 350,000 people on the 200km-long Atlantic coast.

CARIBBEAN COAST

NICARAGUA

PROVINCIA
HEREDIA

Turtle Beach ★

● **Tortuguero**
p. 96

Parque Nacional
★ **Tortuguero**

80km, 3 hrs

PROVINCIA LIMÓN

Guácimo

Guápiles

Matina

Siquirres

COSTA RICA

Pacayas

Turrialba

Cartago

Juan Viñas

El Tejar

Paraíso

PROVINCIA CARTAGO

PROVINCIA
SAN JOSÉ

MARCO POLO HIGHLIGHTS

★ **PARQUE NACIONAL TORTUGUERO**
An unforgettable boat ride through the jungle, perfect for spotting animals. ➤ p. 96

★ **TURTLE BEACH**
In Tortuguero National Park, visitors can (discreetly) watch the turtles laying their eggs. ➤ p. 97

★ **PUERTO VIEJO DE TALAMANCA**
Experience the real Caribbean feeling up close. ➤ p. 99

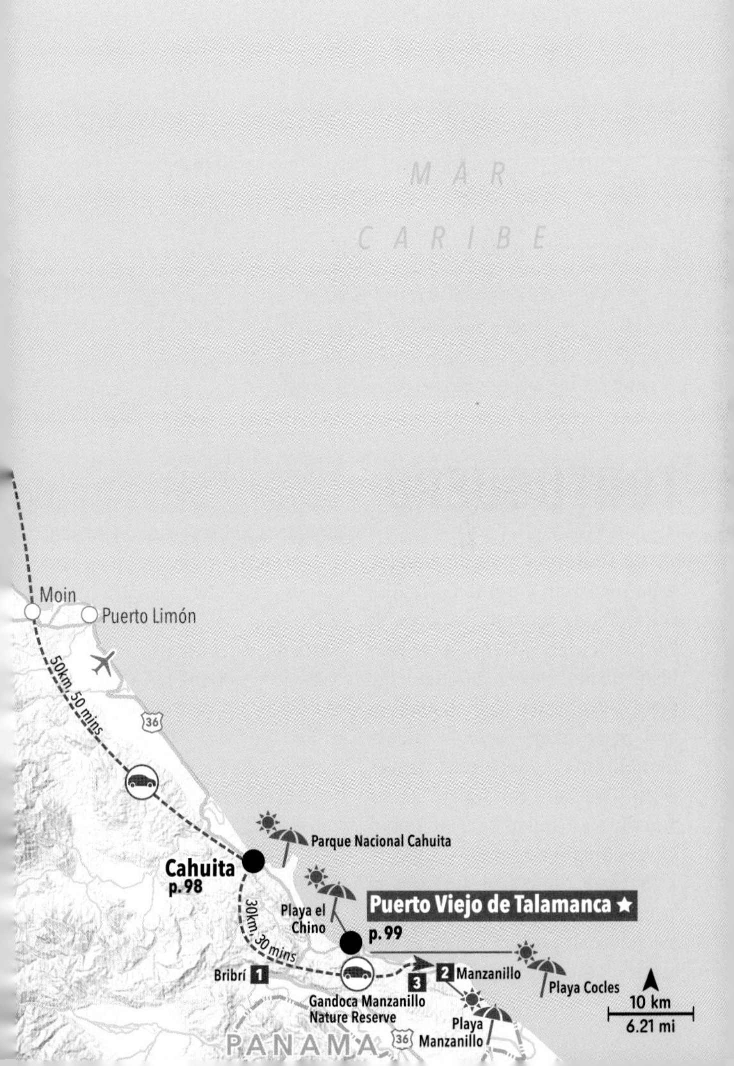

MAR

CARIBE

Moin

Puerto Limón

50 km, 50 miles

36

Parque Nacional Cahuita

Cahuita
p. 98

Playa el Chino

30 km, 30 mins

Puerto Viejo de Talamanca ★
p. 99

Bribrí **1**

Gandoca Manzanillo
Nature Reserve

36

3 **2** Manzanillo

Playa
Manzanillo

Playa Cocles

10 km
6.21 mi

PANAMA

The *tortuga* is both the star and namesake of the Tortuguero National Park

TORTUGUERO

(□ K3) **One of the most memorable experiences on a trip to Costa Rica is the ⚑ ride through the large ★ Parque Nacional Tortuguero. Your boat glides slowly through the deep green water, past mangroves and palm trees. Sunlight breaks through the overhanging leaves, white ibis and parrots fly above, and the air is full of a sweet humidity and the sounds of the jungle.**

The park consists of a system of lagoons and canals that are travelled in traditional tree trunk canoes as well as on bigger boats. The wildlife reserve is home to big mammals, such as manatees, as well as reptiles and hundreds of bird species. Ocelot and jaguar hunt in the inaccessible, humid forests, and temperatures around 30°C and frequent rainfall have created exceptionally species-rich vegetation, even by Costa Rican standards.

Tortuga means tortoise, and the park's beaches are a breeding ground for turtles. From July until October, the pregnant females – including the 200kg green sea turtle – swim to the shore on moonlit nights to lay their eggs. Tortuguero is accessible from Moín, 7km west of Puerto Limón (□ L5), by boat on canals that run north, parallel to the coast, in around three hours. It is also possible to get here by water from La Pavona near Cariari or from Caño Blanco near Siquirres, and by air from San José.

SIGHTSEEING

TURTLE BEACH ★
The park was opened in 1975 for the protection of the endangered green sea turtle, the hawksbill turtle and the leatherback turtle. From July to October, the heavy creatures crawl onto the beach at night to lay their eggs in the sand. They return to the water before the merciless sun reappears. All lodges and hotels offer observation tours to see the night-time egg-laying. Otherwise, you can book a tour at the kiosk of the *Asociación de Guías de Tortuguero* in Tortuguero village.

EATING & DRINKING

Almost all lodges have restaurants, and meals are usually included in the price. There are cafés, *sodas* and restaurants in the village. Why not order *rondón caribeño*, exotically flavoured fish soup, grilled prawns wrapped in coconut, or jerk chicken (marinated and cooked on a wood fire).

INSIDER TIP
Taste Afro-Caribbean dishes

BUDDA CAFÉ
Sundowners, salads and pizzas in a cool atmosphere, with a touch of Ibiza and a hippie feel, right by the sea. *C/ Principal, 25m north of the jetty | tel. 27 09 80 84 | buddahomecafe. com | $$*

TAYLOR'S PLACE
The place to be after sunset in Tortuguero village: candles, palm fronds rustling in the breeze, and delicious rum and coconut cocktails. Owner Ray Taylor serves the best shrimps and steaks (with tamarind sauce) in the area. *Little Street | tel. 87 31 97 89 | $$*

SPORT & ACTIVITIES

BOAT TRIPS
A ride on the waterways is one of the best ways to experience nature here.

SAVING TURTLES

As the digging up and selling of turtle eggs is still widespread in Costa Rica, many tourists act as "rescuers". They are not allowed to touch the eggs or change their position, but they are able to watch and ensure that the hatchlings don't fall into the wrong hands. The baby turtles then make their own way directly into the safety of the water, with around 40 per cent having a chance of survival.

The "egg run" begins here in July. It is organised by wildlife conservation organisations with the help of volunteers.

Chilling in Cahuita: a relaxed atmosphere with young people and music

The branches of the palm trees hang down to the water, exotic birds flit from shore to shore, and monkeys swing from the trees. The individual lodges all have boats of various sizes that they use to explore the rivers, lagoons and canals of the national park. This is usually done in small groups with an experienced guide. However, it is also possible to hire smaller boats for individual excursions, and you can find various canoe and kayak hire places in Tortuguero village.

CAHUITA

(□ M6) **The village of Cahuita (population 3,000) is the gateway to the Caribbean, where unspoilt, wildlife-rich nature awaits. It's ideal for swimming in the clear Caribbean waters and as a starting point for adventures and expeditions in the hinterland.**

A palm-fringed road, with the beach to the left, banana plantations to the right, plus red achiote trees whose fruits were used as dye by the pre-Columbian population, runs into the village of Cahuita. Music and conviviality are the order of the day here. However, the centre of the town, with the north entrance to the Cahuita National Park, has basic hotels, *cabinas* and restaurants, and has remained rather quiet overall.

Nowhere else in Costa Rica can you see so many animals and such lush vegetation in the wild as here. It is only logical that it has to rain for this ecosystem to function well. Evergreen nature also dominates the entire, deep hinterland and accompanies you all the way to the border with Panama in the south.

The atmospheric part of the Caribbean begins in Cahuita, where the first reggae bars and typical Caribbean restaurants await you. You might get the impression that Bob Marley was the only reggae artist to exist – you'll hear his music everywhere you go.

SIGHTSEEING

PARQUE NACIONAL CAHUITA ✈
Costa Rica's second oldest national park has impressive fauna and flora, with swamp and mangrove forest, toucans, hummingbirds and ara parrots, plus monkeys, raccoons and sloths. It also has wonderful white beaches and turquoise seas – a habitat for schools of tropical fish.

Fabulous beaches stretch from Cahuita across the peninsula. The well-prepared, 8km-long, main trail leads through the forest, parallel to the coast and beach. There are numerous excellent bathing spots, the best of which are pretty much halfway along the route. Just don't leave your belongings unattended: the monkeys here are not too particular about private property.

There is a free entrance to the national park from 🐗 Kelly Creek, although donations are always gratefully received. At the second access point, Puerto Vargas, where you'll walk for the first 2km along a raised track over a dark swamp, an entrance fee of $5.65 is charged. *Daily 8am–4pm, last admission 2pm | sinac.go.cr*

EATING & DRINKING

EL CANGREJO LOCO
Good atmosphere and frequent live music. There is something for everyone on the menu: from Caribbean chicken to *chalupas* (tortillas topped with meat, sauce and cheese) and pizza. *Village centre | tel. 88 22 38 44 | $$*

REGGAE BAR
The perfect place for an ice-cold beer with the right rhythms, accompanied by all kinds of delicacies from the sea. *At Playa Negra | tel. 88 12 43 95 | $$*

SPORT & ACTIVITIES
Bird-watching, horse-riding, tree-climbing and zip-lining in the tree canopy are offered at the *Selva Bananito Lodge (tel. 22 53 81 18 | selvabananito.com)*, 40km northwest of Cahuita. You can even get a bird's eye view of

INSIDER TIP
High above the forest

the land on a gyrocopter flight with pilot Juergen. Directions: turn inland off the N36 1km north of the bridge over the Río Vizcaya.

PUERTO VIEJO DE TALAMANCA

(▢ M6) **Good vibes are in the air: the colourful, lively resort of ★ Puerto Viejo (population 3,500),**

with countless hotels, restaurants and bars, plus a wonderful, quiet and white beach, is a meeting place for travellers of all ages.

Music is a key element of the town's appeal. The hot days are spent playing volleyball on the beach, surfing, swimming and – between December and April – scuba diving. The fish-rich sea is warm and invites you to swim and snorkel.

SIGHTSEEING

CENTRO DE RESCATE JAGUAR 🐾

Well worth a visit – especially with children – is the Jaguar Rescue Centre, a sanctuary for orphaned and injured wild animals 5km southeast in Punta Cocles. The name is misleading, as jaguars have never lived here, but nature conservation is omnipresent. Sweet: they also look after orphaned baby sloths. We recommend you buy tickets online in advance. *Guided tours only: daily 9.30am and 11.30am | jaguarrescue.com | ⏱ 1½ hrs*

EATING & DRINKING

A number of excellent small restaurants line the narrow streets of this friendly village. Here you can enjoy a marvellous feast.

GROW

If you haven't tried it, it's hard to imagine that vegetarian and vegan food can be made so delicious – the chicken nuggets made from mushrooms are a dream. The restaurant is right on Playa el Chino, with fantastic views and sometimes even more fantastic sunsets *Tel. 86 21 73 37 | $$$*

SALSA BRAVA

Dany and his family are a local institution and their place is always open. The atmosphere is good from breakfast onwards. The menu is great and varied, but it takes a little while to get served. The party starts at midnight. *On the beach in the town centre | tel. 27 50 31 96 | $$*

SPICY COCONUT

In a perfect beach location on Playa Cocles, you can sample all kinds of delicacies at Spicy Coconut. The Asian specialities are particularly recommended because they are simply delicious. Please note that some dishes are extremely hot! *5km outside town at east end of Playa Cocles, same access as Hotel Villas de Caribe | tel. 22 01 78 49 | spicy-coconut.com | $$*

SPORT & ACTIVITIES

SURFING

Just south of the village you will find *Salsa Brava*, the local name for one of the most notorious surf spots on the coast. It is considered the most difficult wave in the whole of Costa Rica – definitely only for professionals. Beginners stay close to the village, while advanced surfers head for nearby Playa Cocles – but watch out for the currents here.

INSIDER TIP
You, Hershel and a board

Fancy learning how to surf? Local pro Hershel will teach you how to catch the right wave *(private lessons from $55 | tel. 83 57 77 03 | puertoviejosurfandtours.com)*. Hershel also runs a project helping destitute young people from the neighbouring villages to develop a love of nature and confidence in the world through surfing.

BEACHES

The southern Caribbean surpasses itself, with every beach seeming more beautiful than the last. Even the gleaming white 🏖 beaches of Puerto Viejo, 🌴 *Playa el Chino* and *Playa Puerto Viejo*, invite you to swim – or rather splash around – in the mostly shallow water. Ideal for families.

The sections to the east are fantastic. First comes the mile-long 🌴 *Playa Cocles*, with terrific surf but also dangerous currents, so be careful. An endless row of hotels and restaurants line the shore, and the choice is stunning. This is followed by *Playa Chasma*, *Playa Escondida*, *Playa Chiquita*, *Playa Punta Uva* and *Playa Grande*, which finally merges into *Playa Manzanillo*. In between are small, partly shallow bays – deserted miles of beach, the quintessential Caribbean.

Puerto Viejo's beaches are great for splashing around, sunbathing, sports and just relaxing

AROUND PUERTO VIEJO

1 BRIBRÍ

14km southwest of Puerto Viejo / 20 mins

The town is home to the indigenous Talamanca people, who work hard at harvest time for little remuneration, and is a destination for travellers interested in the culture of the *indígenas*. The village, with basic wooden houses surrounded by banana plantations, lies on the Panama border, and with its surrounding area is designated as a reservation. The meeting place is the turquoise *Restaurante Bribrí (tel. 27 51 00 44 | $)*. 📖 *M6*

2 MANZANILLO

15km east of Puerto Viejo / 20 mins

From Puerto Viejo, the coastal road continues in a southeasterly direction, where it ends after 15km in Playa Manzanillo. Remote, palm-fringed beaches, fishing boats and reggae music emanating from cafés and colourful wooden houses: fans of authentic Afro-Caribbean atmosphere love this small settlement. You quickly get the feeling that there is room for holidaymakers in every house: there are some classy hostels and numerous other types of accommodation in the middle and lower price brackets. In Manzanillo, everyone travels in a leisurely manner by bicycle, mostly on heavy models without any gears. This is also the ideal way for you to explore the surrounding area, and bike hire can be found on every corner of the town. You won't experience any stress here, just chill out on the beautiful 🌴 *Playa Manzanillo*, explore the area and enjoy an evening beer with a view of the waves. At the end of the day, *Colores Restaurant & Beach Lounge (100m behind the town sign on Playa Manzanillo | tel. 62 03 07 98 | FB | $$$)*, right on the beach, offers excellent service and good food prepared by Greek immigrants – it's warm and rustic. They also have an incredible drinks menu, with the finest wines from all over the world.

> **INSIDER TIP**
> **An outstanding drinks menu**

If you still feel like turning your back on the beach, *Ara Manzanillo (between Playa Punta Uva and Playa Grande, 400m south of the junction | tel. 89 71 14 36 | aramanzanillo.org)*, is a project dedicated to reintroducing a population of green macaws to the area and thus contributing to the conservation of this species. It's well worth supporting, and its efforts are working! There are already 120 of these majestic birds living in the area again. There is a lot of activity in the trees when the daily feeding takes place at 3pm *(⏱ 1–1½ hrs)* Visitors pay $20 to keep the project alive. 📖 *N6*

Hiking trail in the Gandoca Manzanillo Nature Reserve

3 GANDOCA MANZANILLO NATURE RESERVE

18km southeast of Puerto Viejo / 20 mins by car to Manzanillo, then 1½ hrs on foot

Where the road ends at a river, this little-explored nature reserve begins, and it stretches all the way to Panama. There are regular buses from Puerto Viejo to Manzanillo. Alternatively you can take a tuk-tuk for around 10,000 colones (around $20). If you then walk from Manzanillo along the sea for around 5km to Punta Mona (which is beautiful!) or take a boat for $10 per person, you will reach a largely intact coral reef, where schools of fish and fantastic vegetation await. *N6*

INSIDER TIP
Snorkelling paradise

WHERE TO STAY ON THE CARIBBEAN COAST

JUNGLE LUXURY

The *Namú Garden Hotel & Spa (tel. 87 89 60 70 | namuhotelpuerto viejo.com | $$$)* in Puerto Viejo de Talamanca is outstanding. There are 22 luxurious rooms and suites right on the edge of the village, but already in the jungle, plus a restaurant (modern Caribbean cuisine) and wellness facilities.

BY THE LAGOON

The exquisitely managed *Mawamba Lodge (54 rooms | tel. 22 93 81 81 | mawamba.com | $$)* in Tortuguero is in a wild, fantastically beautiful location between a canal and the Caribbean. Guests can expect both a beach and a private jetty for tours through the labyrinth of canals.

DISCOVERY TOURS

Want to get under the skin of this country? Then our discovery tours are the ideal guide – they provide advice on which sights to visit, tips on where to stop for that perfect holiday snap, a choice of the best places to eat and drink, and suggestions for fun activities.

❶ FROM SAN JOSÉ THROUGH NATIONAL PARKS TO THE CARIBBEAN COAST

➤ At eye level with the rainforest canopy
➤ Cruise along jungle canals
➤ Smell the scents of the tropical forest

San José	Tortuguero
→ approx. 135km	3 days, driving time (without stops) 4½ hours

GLIDE THROUGH THE JUNGLE

From the Terminal del Caribe bus terminal (C/ Central/Av. 13–15) in ❶ San José ➤ p. 44, *take the early morning*

DAY 1
❶ San José

Your destination on tour No.2: the dream-like beaches of Parque Nacional Manuel Antonio

bus via Guápiles to Cariari, and begin at the ❷ Parque Nacional Braulio Carrillo ➤ p. 51. *Shortly after going through the Zurquí Tunnel, the bus crosses the Río Sucio. A few minutes later (5km past the bridge), on the right is the access point to the almost legendary* Aerial Tram ➤ p. 52 *in the rainforest, known by the locals as the teleférico ("cable car"). Get off the bus and enjoy the ride through the jungle. Allow at least three hours. Once your ride is finished, a cable car employee will help you find the correct bus to Cariari. At Guápiles the N247 branches off north to Cariari.* Spend the night at the ❸ Hotel Vista al Tortuguero *(info@hotelvista tortuguero.com).*

FROM HERE IT'S BY BOAT ONLY

From Cariari, take the 2pm bus to ❹ La Pavona *30km to the north* – *a bumpy ride lasting around an hour. The bus drops you off at the harbour pier, where flat-bottomed motorboats will be waiting for your almost hour-long trip through the canals of the Río de la Suerte and on into the Río Penetencia, two rivers rich in wildlife, travelling as far as the canals of Tortuguero near the village of the same name. On the way, rainforest slowly replaces a landscape characterised by banana*

| 35km |
| ❷ Parque Nacional Braulio Carrillo |
| 52km |
| ❸ Hotel Vista al Tortuguero |
| DAY 2 |
| 30km |
| ❹ La Pavona |

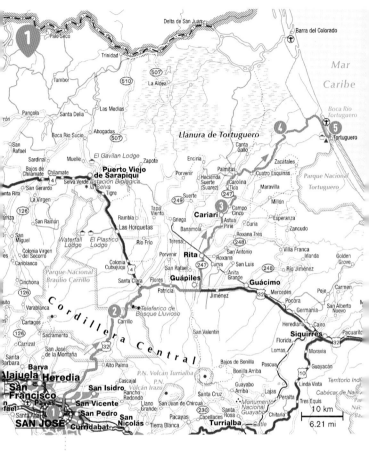

16km

⑤ Tortuguero

cultivation and cattle farming, and you will spot the first crocodiles. *From the jetty, it's a five-minute walk to the car-free zone of* ⑤ Tortuguero ➤ p.96. Once there, *walk north to* Miss Junie's jetty. Junie and her daughters Noli and Dorly have been here for what feels like forever and will let you in on the secrets of this exciting landscape – they are practically the story here. Miss Junie's Lodge *(reservationmissjunie@gmail.com)* also offers good and affordable accommodation.

PURE NATURE

Tortuguero offers numerous options for excursions – the next day can be filled with hikes and paddling in the rivers, canals and lagoons. You will be awoken by the noises of the jungle, learn all sorts of interesting facts about the area on a guided tour, and get close views of howler monkeys, turtles and crocodiles.

DAY 3

❷ FROM SAN JOSÉ TO THE PACIFIC

➤ Explore the Carara National Park on hiking trails
➤ Canal trip into the mangroves
➤ At the Mariposa Hotel: an addictive view!

📍 San José

➡ 190km

🏁 La Mariposa Hotel

🚗 3 days, driving time (without stops) 4 hours

PARROTS AND PUMAS

On the highway (Route 27) you'll travel west from ❶ San José ➤ p. 44 *through the Valle Central and the little town of Orotina. A few more miles to the south is the beginning of the* ❷ Parque Nacional Carara ➤ p. 83, home to jaguars, pumas and ocelots. Look forward to monkeys and wonderfully coloured tropical birds, including giant ara parrots. Trails take you further into the national park.

BY THE SEA

Welcome to the sea! The route from the capital to the central Pacific is one of the busiest in the coastal region – after all, the capital's inhabitants are also hungry for sunshine and don't want to sit in their cars forever. However, the further south you go, the more spectacular the scenery becomes. *The road (Route 34) now takes you along the coast, crosses the river of the same name at Parrita and wends its way inland for a few miles before ending in a bay at* ❸ Quepos ➤ p. 84, the destination of this journey, where you need to look for accommodation for the next few days.

DAY 1
❶ San José
90km
❷ Parque Nacional Carara

88km

❸ Quepos

WATCH OUT: MONKEYS FROM ABOVE!

Go to Cambute Mangrove Tours *(tel. 27 77 32 29 | cambutemangrovetourscr.com)* for a boat ride through the canals of the Isla Damas estuary. Keep a close eye on your bag – little monkeys might hop on

INSIDER TIP
Watch your bag!

board as you pass under trees. *Moving on, a narrow road winds its way from Quepos 7km up the mountain and back down again.* There are restaurants and lodges in tropical gardens on the slopes on both sides of the road. You'll have a panoramic view of the Manuel Antonio National Park and its islands from ➍ Emilio's Café *(Ctra. a Manuel Antonio km 4 (at the Plaza Vista Shopping) | tel. 27 77 68 07 | $$).*

5km

➍ Emilio's Café

108

Finish your tour with dinner at La Mariposa

The next day is for exploring the famous ⑤ Parque Nacional Manuel Antonio ➤ p. 85. *At the end of the road, before you get to the park,* is the Manuel Antonio settlement, with beautiful beaches that invite you to bathe. Along the riverside road, which is only a sandy track here, long-term travellers sit in the cafés as Indian batiks and amulets flap in the wind. End the day on the terrace of ⑥ La Mariposa Hotel *(lamariposa.com)*: with the sea and national park at your feet. Fabulous!

DAY 3
3km
⑤ Parque Nacional Manuel Antonio
3km
⑥ La Mariposa Hotel

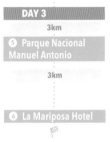

③ ON FOOT THROUGH THE CURI-CANCHA CLOUD FOREST

➤ An adventure on narrow paths through the wilderness
➤ Share experiences with other travellers over a cup of coffee
➤ Test your vision: how many animals can you spot?

📍	Santa Elena	🏁	Santa Elena
🔄	4km	🥾	1 day, walking time (without stops) 4 hours
📊	very easy	↗	180m

ℹ Only 50 people are allowed into Curi-Cancha at any one time, so be at the entrance as early as possible. You will also need to show your passport or a copy.

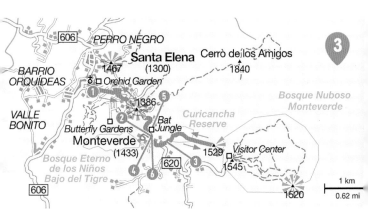

Take the shuttle bus from ❶ Santa Elena to Monteverde and get off at Casem, a women's co-operative for art and crafts. Fortify yourself with breakfast at ❷ Stella's Monteverde *(daily from 8am | tel. 26 45 55 60 | stellas monteverde.com)* café-restaurant across the road. *Then walk along the gravel road which, at the Cheese Factory approx. 300m further to the southeast, branches off eastbound to the Curi-Cancha nature reserve.* The ❸ Reserva Curi-Cancha *(reservacuricancha.com)* is open daily from 7am–3pm, and from 6–8pm for guided night hikes *(caminata nocturna).*

❶ Santa Elena

2,5km

❷ Stella's Monteverde

500m

❸ Reserva
Curi-Cancha

THE MESMERISING JUNGLE

Seven signposted trails cover the hilly terrain: *take the path to the Mirador a la División Continental lookout.* A guided tour is recommended. This way, you will get to see all the things you would have missed otherwise, such as the roots of a strangler fig, singing bellbirds, rare quetzals in avocado trees, toucans, or spider monkeys tumbling around the treetops. From the Mirador a la División Continental you overlook the continental divide: to the west, rivers flow into the Pacific, to the east into the Atlantic. After three hours – full of information, short breaks and looking for things with binoculars – you'll be back at the entrance.

Lunch is at ④ Casem ➤ p. 69. Then it's on to the ⑤ Bat Jungle *(daily 9am–5pm | batjungle.com)* nearby, right behind Stella's. A large darkened enclosure is home to some 90 bats, and you can get right up close to them on a 45-minute tour. Then it's back into the sun and time to rummage through the shelves at ⑥ Casem for that exceptional souvenir for your friends at home. If you miss the last shuttle bus back to ① Santa Elena, one of the nice *señoritas* at Casem will be pleased to call you a taxi.

3 km

④ Casem
150 m
⑤ Bat Jungle
150 m
⑥ Casem
2,5 km
① Santa Elena

As if in another world: a mysterious aura surrounds the cloud forest

GOOD TO KNOW

HOLIDAY BASICS

ARRIVAL

GETTING THERE

British Airways *(britishairways.com)* offers direct flights from London to San José with a journey time of just under 11 hours. Flights from the UK with stopovers are available with various airlines to both San José and Liberia. US airlines such as Delta, United and American offer flights from US cities to Costa Rica, some of them direct. Direct flight times are usually under six hours. You can get non-stop flights from Toronto with Air Canada, which take just over five hours.

The (orange) airport taxi to San José costs $35–$40, to Heredia $40–$45 and to Alajuela $11–$22. The only airport bus runs to Alajuela (approx. $1.20), where you have to change to your next destination.

IMMIGRATION

British citizens do not need a visa to enter Costa Rica and may stay for up to 180 days under a tourist visa waiver. Your passport should have an expiry date at least one day after the day you plan to leave. US passport-holders also do not require an entry visa to Costa Rica, but need a current valid passport and a return ticket to exit Costa Rica within 90 days.

GETTING AROUND

DRIVING & CAR HIRE

A national driving licence is sufficient for holiday visitors. When driving off the main roads and in national parks, you'll need a vehicle with a four-wheel drive *(doble tracción)*. Some of the

Costa Rica: a chance to drive an SUV without too much of a guilty conscience

GMT minus 6 hours, and minus 7 hours during British Summer Time

 Adapter Type A

110 volt mains voltage, US-style flat plugs.

roads are very poor, and even dangerous due to deep potholes. You will encounter frequent road closures and lengthy detours. There are often no signposts, and the *Ticos* drive recklessly. During the rainy season, roads are sometimes impassable. Therefore, get your facts right before setting off and drive defensively! A navigation system on your smartphone is useful, such as *Waze (waze.com)*; you need a permanent internet connection to use it. Google Maps does not work reliably in Costa Rica. You should not travel in the dark. The speed limit outside built-up areas is 80km/h, on some highways up to 110km/h.

Hire cars are available from around $45 per day (incl. taxes and fully comprehensive insurance), and an off-road vehicle can quickly cost considerably more. All defects are entered in a checklist, which you should check carefully. This is because dubious hire companies, which even appear on the major booking portals, like to charge for scratches and dents when you return the vehicle. We recommend booking through a well-known provider such as Adobe, Alamo or amiGo before travelling. If you hire a car, you should also take out luggage insurance. When travelling, park the vehicle in a guarded car park.

DOMESTIC FLIGHTS

Sansa Air (flysansa.com) flies with propeller aircraft from Juan Santamaría International Airport in San José to 11 destinations in the country. Tickets usually cost $60–$130.

PUBLIC TRANSPORT

Buses connect the capital, San José, to all the towns and every part of the country. They are extremely reasonable, but often packed, especially at the weekends. The private companies have their own stations (more than ten in San José), and a bus timetable *(at visitcostarica.com/es/costa-rica/bus-itinerary)* provides information on their locations and destinations. For long-distance destinations and weekend travel, it's best to purchase your tickets in advance. The private company *Interbus (interbusonline.com)* operates 12-seater minibuses to all the tourist destinations daily.

There are also lots of ferries around the Gulf of Nicoya and across the estuary of the Río Tempisque. There is a ferry connection to the Península de Osa from Golfito to Puerto Jiménez and a ferry to Rincón.

TAXIS

Taxi rides can be annoying in Costa Rica, especially in San José. If the meter *(maría)* is on, then journeys are very cheap, but this is rare. Drivers don't switch it on, or fail to reset it so that the previous amount is included in your fare. The *maría* might have been manipulated (you'll hear a loud clicking), or the driver may tell you it's broken. It is less complicated to use *Uber (uber.com), as* you can see what the journey will cost in advance. Install the app at home, as it may not be possible to do so when you are travelling.

EMERGENCIES

EMBASSIES
BRITISH EMBASSY IN SAN JOSÉ
Edificio Centro Colón | Paseo Colón / Streets 38 and 40, Apartado 815 –1007 | tel. +506 2258 2025 (from Costa Rica) or 020 7008 1500 (from the UK) | gov.uk/world/organisations/british-embassy-in-costa-rica

US EMBASSY IN SAN JOSÉ
Calle 98 Vía 104 | Pavas | tel. (506) 2519-2000 | cr.usembassy.gov

EMBASSY OF CANADA IN SAN JOSÉ
Behind the "Contraloría" in the Oficentro Ejecutivo La Sabana | Building 5, Third floor | tel. 0 800 015 1161

RESPONSIBLE TRAVEL

It doesn't take a lot to be environmentally friendly while travelling. Consider your carbon footprint when flying to and from your holiday destination *(myclimate.org, routerank.com)*, and how you can protect nature and culture abroad. As a tourist, it is especially important to respect nature, look out for local products, cycle instead of drive, save water and much more. To find out more, see *ecotourism.org*.

FESTIVALS & EVENTS
ALL YEAR ROUND

FEBRUARY

Día de la Candelaria (particularly elaborate in Paraíso near Cartago): Candlemas, 2 February. Plays, concerts, music and dance in honour of the Virgin Mary.

Fiesta de los Diablitos (Rey Curré): The "Festival of the Little Devils". Flute and drum music accompany locals wearing decorative balsa-wood masks commemorating battles between the indigenous people and the Spanish (photo). A similar event takes place in Boruca village over the new year.

Envision Festival (Uvita), *envision festival.com:* Several thousand visitors party to electronic music, do yoga and take part in esoteric workshops.

MARCH/APRIL

Semana Santa (entire country): Holy Week. Since colonial times, Easter has been the country's most important festival, celebrated with processions.

JULY

Fiesta de la Virgen del Mar (Puntarenas): Saturday closest to 16 July. A parade of boats in honour of the Virgin of the Sea processes once round the peninsula in the Gulf of Nicoya.

AUGUST

Nuestra Señora de los Ángeles (Cartago): On Our Lady of the Angels Day (2 August) crowds of pilgrims proceed to the basilica in Cartago.

OCTOBER

Carnival in Puerto Limón: A week of festivities when you can forget about getting any sleep, as the Limonenses parade through the streets accompanied by steel drums and samba-loving visitors.

DECEMBER–JANUARY

Fin del Año (particularly elaborate in the centre of San José): The end of the year is celebrated with horse parades *(topes)*, bullfights *(corridas)* and festive processions.

EMERGENCY SERVICES
General emergency (tel. 911 | also in English). Red Cross (tel. 128).

ESSENTIALS

ACCOMMODATION
Hotel prices vary greatly between the seasons, dropping by almost half between May and October, in the rainy season ("green season"). In recent years, international four- and five-star hotels have opened in various towns in the highlands, as well as near popular beaches. Overall, though, the country continues to attract people who prefer rustic lodges and small, independent guesthouses. You can find youth hostels and cheap accommodation at *hostelworld.com/hostels/costarica.*

ADDRESSES
Not all the streets have names, instead you'll see something like "100m south of XX Park". House numbers are almost non-existent, and the relevant corner is given instead: Av. 4/C/ 5 means "Avenida 4, corner Calle 5"; or C/ 2/Av. 2–4 (even shorter: c2, a2/4) means "2nd road between Avenidas 2 and 4".

ADMISSION FEES
Admission fees to national and adventure parks vary between $15 and $160. Activities are extra. If you want to see the cloud forest from above, for example, you will have to pay up to $70 for a canopy tour. Children and teenagers usually get a discount, and the former sometimes even get free

entry. Larger museums cost around $10, and the fantastic *Museo del Oro Precolombino* in San José charges $16.

HOW MUCH DOES IT COST?

Coffee	$1.70–$2.30 *for one cup*
Snack	$2–$2.30 *for one gallo*
Beer	$2.30 *for one bottle*
Gifts	$17–$35 *for a cotton hammock*
Petrol	*around* $1.15 *for 1 litre petrol*
National park	$6–$20 *for admission*

CAMPING
Camping is uncommon in Costa Rica. There are only a few campsites and they are usually desolate and unhygienic; hostels are a better budget option.

CUSTOMS
It is permitted to bring 200 cigarettes and 3 litres of alcoholic beverages into Costa Rica, along with items for personal use, without paying duty. Goods valued up to £390 are duty free when entering the UK. They can include 4 litres of spirits and 200 cigarettes. See gov.uk for further details. You can normally take goods to a value of $800 into the USA; see *cbp.gov* for details.

HEALTH
Vaccinations are not mandatory. There is a risk of malaria and dengue fever in

the coastal areas and in regions below 600m. Protect yourself with appropriate clothing, insect repellent and a mosquito net. Tap water is safe throughout Costa Rica and can be used to brush your teeth. However, in remote areas (national parks or the Caribbean) it is safer to use bottled water or boiled tap water. Medical care in the capital is excellent. In an emergency, contact the *Clínica Bíblica (Av. 14/ C/ Central–1 | tel. 25 22 10 00 | clinicabiblica.com)* or *Hospital CIMA (Escazú | tel. 22 08 10 00 | hospitalcima.com)*.

INFORMATION

Costa Rica doesn't have an information office in Europe. Tourist information is available from the *Embassy of Costa Rica (14 Lancaster Gate, London W2 3LH | tel. 020 7706 8844 | costa ricanembassy.co.uk)*. The official Costa Rican tourism organisations ICT (Instituto Costarricense de Turismo) and Canatur (Cámara Nacional de Turismo) have only a few information offices in Costa Rica. In many cases, travel agencies and tour operators have assumed this role. There is plenty of information on the ICT website, *visitcostarica.com*, including in English.

MONEY & CREDIT CARDS

The local currency is the *colón* (100 *céntimos*), but the US dollar is also commonly used. Current exchange rates can be found at websites such as *oanda.com*. Dollar prices generally apply to tourist offers, and *colones* for everything else. It is advisable to pay in the currency charged, otherwise it is usually a little more expensive. Both currencies can be withdrawn by credit card with PIN at ATMs (note the fees!). The state banks *(Banco Nacional* and *Banco de Costa Rica)* have smaller limits per withdrawal (approx. $100), and they often only offer *colones*. Private banks are different, but you will only find them in larger cities or in the central valley. Payment by credit card (Visa, Mastercard) is widespread.

NATIONAL PARKS

Humidity and temperatures are high in the national parks and protected areas. You'll need multi-functional clothing and comfortable hiking boots. Take water and perhaps a snack, as these can usually only be purchased at the entrances to the parks and protected areas. The parks don't like to see plastic bottles, and sometimes they are prohibited. You should always expect rain, so it's a good idea to take a lightweight rain-proof jacket with you. At the Corcovado and Tortuguero parks guides are compulsory. Otherwise you can decide for yourself whether to explore the wilderness alone with a map or whether you would rather have animals and special plants pointed out to you. Each national park has its own opening hours, and some are closed one day a week.

NATURAL HAZARDS

Several of Costa Rica's volcanoes are active, with minor eruptions occurring. Turrialba has been very active for several years. Thanks to an excellent early warning system, the country has a reliable disaster management system. Find out about the current status before travelling. Sometimes affected national parks and roads are closed. As Costa Rica is located on the edge of active tectonic plates, small, generally harmless earth tremors must be expected from time to time. Roads can also be dangerous during heavy rainfall, and there is a risk of landslides. This applies, in particular, to the N32 across the Braulio Carrillo National Park – this route is regularly closed.

PERSONAL SAFETY

Costa Rica is a very safe country to visit. A higher crime rate really only affects the capital, San José, Jacó on the Pacific, and Puerto Limón and Moín on the Caribbean coast. In these locations, there are an increasing number of armed robberies in the evenings and in dark areas. Poverty and unemployment, petty crime and car thefts are also on the rise. Follow these tips to travel safely: don't travel on public buses after dark; don't go alone to an ATM; on day trips, only take as much money with you as you will need, and leave the rest in the hotel safe; never leave valuables in a hire car.

PHONES & MOBILE PHONES

The international dial code for Costa Rica is *00506*. From Costa Rica to the UK the code is *0044*, to the United States *001*. Prepaid SIM cards by Kölbi *(kolbi.cr)* for tourists are available from 3,000 *colones* and obtainable from ICE desks *(ict.go.cr)*. The Costa Rican network providers Claro CR *(claro.cr)* and Liberty *(libertycr.com)* also offer SIM cards *(chip)* for tourists at reasonable rates. Kölbi have the best coverage.

PUBLIC HOLIDAYS

Public holidays are usually on a Monday or Friday, thereby creating a long weekend.

1 Jan	*Año Nuevo* (New Year's Day)
19 March	*Día de San José* (St José's Day)
March/April	*Jueves y Viernes Santo*
	(Maundy Thursday and Good Friday)
11 April	*Juan Santamaría Day*
1 May	*Día del Trabajo* (Labour Day)
29 June	*San Pedro y Pablo*
	(St Peter and Paul's Day)
25 July	*Anexión de Guanacaste*
	(Guanacaste Day)
2 Aug	*Virgen de los Ángeles*
	(Our Lady of the Angels)
15 Aug	*Día de la Madre* (Assumption Day/
	Mothering Sunday)
15 Sept	*Día de la Independencia*
	(Independence Day)
12 Oct	*Día de la Raza* (Columbus Day)
2 Nov	*Día de los Muertos* (All Souls' Day)
8 Dec	*Concepción Inmaculada*
	(Immaculate Conception)
25 Dec	*Navidad* (Christmas)

TIPPING

In restaurants, a service charge is usually included in the bill, but this shouldn't be confused with a tip: you can give up to ten per cent on top of this for good service. In hotels, give cleaning staff and porters around 1,000 *colones* per day or suitcase.

WI-FI

WLAN (Wi-Fi) is available in most hotels and guesthouses. It is also possible to log on for free using a password in many cafés and restaurants in Costa Rica, although access may occasionally be unavailable, especially in remote regions and during the rainy season.

WHEN TO GO

Temperatures remain around the same all year round, with only minor fluctuations between the months. In the highlands the average temperature is around 22°C, on the coasts up to 30°C. Climate change is having an impact on the dry and rainy seasons, but the general rule until recently has been as follows: the dry season in the highlands and on the Pacific side of the continental divide is from November to April. The peak travel season is therefore from December to April, with peaks at Christmas and Easter, with local holidaymakers also travelling in July and August. Costa Rica's rainy season is from May until October. Although it usually only rains in the afternoons, they are pretty impressive downpours. It's humid during this time, and there are not many tourists about. This means prices are lower, and lots of hotels have special offers or are closed. On the Caribbean side, you must also expect rain showers during the dry season.

Tips on travelling for nature and animal lovers: whales arrive on the Pacific coast in January, and lots of birds breed in March/April; orchids flower in March; and the turtles come onto the beaches to lay their eggs between July and October.

WOMEN

In macho Costa Rica, women travelling alone may receive curious looks, and unwanted attention. It's safest not to be out and about in San José and Puerto Limón after dark, nor to be alone on remote beaches.

WEATHER IN SAN JOSÉ

	JAN	FEB	MARCH	APRIL	MAY	JUNE	JULY	AUG	SEPT	OCT	NOV	DEC
Daytime temperature	24°	24°	26°	27°	27°	27°	26°	26°	27°	26°	25°	24°
Night-time temperature	14°	14°	15°	16°	16°	16°	16°	16°	16°	15°	15°	15°
Sunshine hours/day	7	8	8	7	5	4	4	4	5	4	4	6
Water temperature in °C	1	0	1	4	17	20	18	19	20	22	14	4

☀ Sunshine hours/day   🌂 Water temperature in °C

USEFUL PHRASES
IN SPANISH

SMALL TALK

yes/no/maybe	sí/no/quizás
please/thank you	por favor/gracias
Hello!/Goodbye/See you soon	¡Hola!/¡Adiós!/¡Hasta luego!
Good morning/evening/night	¡Buenos días!/¡Buenas tardes!/¡Buenas noches!
Excuse me/sorry!	¡Perdona!/¡Perdone!
May I?	¿Puedo ...?
Sorry?/Could you repeat?	¿Cómo dice?
My name is ...	Me llamo ...
What is your name? (formal/informal)	¿Cómo se llama usted?/¿Cómo te llamas?
I am from ... the UK/USA/Ireland	Soy del Reino Unido/de los Estados Unidos/de Irlanda
I (don't) like this	Esto (no) me gusta.
I would like ... /Do you have ...?	Querría .../¿Tiene usted ...?

SYMBOLS

EATING & DRINKING

The menu, please!	¡El menú, por favor!
expensive/cheap/price	caro/barato/precio
Could you bring ... please?	¿Podría traerme ... por favor?
bottle/jug/glass	botella/jarra/vaso
knife/fork/spoon	cuchillo/tenedor/cuchara
salt/pepper/sugar	sal/pimienta/azúcar
vinegar/oil/milk/lemon	vinagre/aceite/leche/limón
cold/too salty/undercooked	frío/demasiado salado/sin hacer
with/without ice/fizz (in water)	con/sin hielo/gas
vegetarian/allergy	vegetariano/vegetariana/alergía
I would like to pay, please	Quiero pagar, por favor.
bill/receipt/tip	cuenta/recibo/propina

MISCELLANEOUS

Where is ...?/Where are ...?	¿Dónde está ...? /¿Dónde están ...?
What time is it?	¿Qué hora es?
today/tomorrow/yesterday	hoy/mañana/ayer
How much is ...?	¿Cuánto cuesta ...?
Where can I get internet/WiFi?	¿Dónde encuentro un acceso a internet/wifi?
Help!/Look out!/Be careful!	¡Socorro!/¡Atención!/¡Cuidado!
pharmacy/drug store	farmacia/droguería
broken/it's not working	roto/no funciona
broken down/garage	avería/taller
Can I take photos here?	¿Puedo fotografiar aquí?
open/closed/opening hours	abierto/cerrado/horario
entrance/exit	entrada/salida
toilets (women/men)	aseos (señoras/caballeros)
(not) drinking water	agua (no) potable
breakfast/B&B/all inclusive	desayuno/media pensión/pensión completa
car park/multi-storey car park	parking/garaje
I would like to hire ...	Quiero alquilar ...
a car/a bike/a boat	un coche/una bicicleta/un barco
0/1/2/3/4/5/6/7/8/9/10/100/1000	cero/un, uno, una/dos/tres/cuatro/cinco/seis/siete/ocho/nueve/diez/cien, ciento/mil

HOLIDAY VIBES
FOR RELAXATION & CHILLING

FOR BOOKWORMS & FILM BUFFS

📖 MONKEYS ARE MADE OF CHOCOLATE

Naturalist Jack Ewing explores the way plants and animals interact with each other in the incredibly diverse ecosystems of Costa Rica's rainforests, with insights gained through decades living in the country's southwest.

🎥 POR LAS PLUMAS – ALL ABOUT THE FEATHERS

This tongue-in-cheek comedy (2013) by Neto Villalobos focuses on the prestige object of ordinary people in Costa Rica: a fighting cock.

📖 A NATURALIST'S GUIDE TO THE BIRDS OF COSTA RICA

Currently probably the best guide to birdwatching, with great photos and catchy texts by Steve Bird. Available locally everywhere.

🎥 JURASSIC WORLD 3: DOMINION

In this cinema blockbuster (2022), the eccentric billionaire's dinosaur zoo is located on a fictitious island off the coast of Costa Rica: Isla Nublar. The film was directed by Colin Trevorrow. Tremendous nature scenes!

PLAYLIST ON SHUFFLE

🔀 ⏮ ⏸ ⏭ 🔊 ─────────

0:58

⏸ **DEBI NOVA** – CUPIDO
Light and full of *pura vida* vibes – you can hear Debi round the clock, from morning with a *café con leche* to late at night in a club.

▶ **WALTER FERGUSON** – CABIN IN THE WATA
The soft voice, the cool intonation and the witty and curious lyrics: an exceptional song by the calypso legend.

▶ **MANUEL TURIZO & OZUNA** – CARAMELO
This is playing in the clubs.

▶ **GANDHI** –ESTRÉLLAME
From the iconic Costa Rican rock band.

▶ **KAROL G** – AY, DIOS MÍO
The Colombian singer's catchy tune will sweeten your day – chilled, harmonious and passionate, it captures the attitude to life of young *Ticos*.

Your holiday soundtrack can be found on **Spotify** under **MARCO POLO Costa Rica**

Or scan this code with the Spotify app

ONLINE

ANIMALS OF COSTA RICA
This free app shows more than 6,000 mammals, reptiles, birds and insects in over 10,000 photos. The most comprehensive nature guide for your trip – what you don't find here doesn't exist in Costa Rica.

BIRDSOUNDS COSTA RICA
This app features over 2,000 tracks of some 800 species of Costa Rican birds

COSTARICA.COM/BLOG
Impressive travel descriptions of the country's various regions and topics.

COSTARICATRAVELBLOG.COM
Trip-planning, discounts, recommendations for experiences and more on this long-standing and informative blog, run by a Costa Rican–US couple.

THECOSTARICANEWS.COM
Local news in English, as well as travel and lifestyle features, and information on festivals and events.

TRAVEL PURSUIT

THE MARCO POLO HOLIDAY QUIZ

Do you know your facts about Costa Rica? Here you can test your knowledge of the little secrets and idiosyncrasies of this country and its people. You will find the correct answers in the footer and in detail on pages 20 to 25 of this guide.

❶ Why are bananas often covered in blue bags on the trees?
a) To protect them from thieving monkeys
b) The blue bags are filled with insecticide
c) To accelerate the ripening process

❷ Why did indigenous people make giant stone spheres?
a) To roll down on enemies
b) To grind grain
c) To recreate the alignment of the stars

❸ What or who are *Ticas*?
a) Women and girls from Costa Rica
b) Supporters of the Costa Rican Liberal Party
c) The mosquitoes on the Caribbean coast

❹ The country's borders in the west and east are the ...
a) ... Caribbean and Atlantic
b) ... Pacific and Caribbean
c) ... Pacific and Gulf of Mexico

❺ Where do most of the 500,000 to one million immigrants in Costa Rica come from?
a) Nicaragua
b) Venezuela
c) Panama

What were these ancient stone spheres used for? See question 2.

❻ What causes turtles' eggs to hatch?
a) The turtles
b) The moon
c) The sun

❼ How many Costa Ricans are indigenous?
a) About 1.5 per cent
b) A good 10 per cent
c) Just under a fifth

❽ How many active and extinct volcanoes are there in Costa Rica?
a) 50
b) 70
c) 120

❾ How many national parks are there in Costa Rica?
a) 9
b) 18
c) 30

❿ Which of these features apply to the Costa Rican state?
a) In elections, parents have one vote for each underage child
b) There is no army
c) There is no income tax

⓫ What percentage of the world's animal and plant species live in the Costa Rica tropical rainforest?
a) Almost 20 per cent
b) Just under a third
c) More than half

⓬ Which export product is of economic importance alongside bananas and coffee?
a) Precious woods
b) Tea
c) Natural gas

INDEX

Aerial Tram (Parque Nacional Braulio Carrillo) 12, 52, 105
Alajuela 53, 112
Alma de Café (San José) 10, 45
Alturas Wildlife Sanctuary 87
Arenal Natura Ecological Park 71
Arenal Volcano 25, 70
Bahía Drake (Península de Osa) 88, 91
Basílica de los Ángeles (Cartago) 57
Bosque Eterno de los Niños (Monteverde) 12, 67
Braulio Carillo National Park (Parque Nacional Braulio Carrillo) 13
Bribrí 102
Butterfly Conservatory (Laguna de Arenal) 13, 71
Cahuita 98
Caldera 35
Caño Blanco 97
Cariari 105
Cartago 56, 115
Casa del Soñador (Valle Orosí) 11, 61
Centro de Rescate Jaguar (Puerto Viejo de Talamanca) 12, 100
Cerro de la Muerte 88
Cerros de Escazú 48
Chirripó 21
Cordillera Central 22
Costa Ballena 86
Doka Estate 10, 55
Ecocentro Danaus (La Fortuna) 71
El Trapiche (Monteverde) 66
Escazú 44
Espadilla Sur 85
Finca Agroecológica La Flor 59
Finca Café Britt (Heredia) 50
Flamingo 37
Gandoca Manzanillo Nature Reserve 103
Golfito 90, 114
Golfo Dulce 37, 90
Guaitil 74
Guayabo National Monument 60
Gulf of Nicoya 114
Heredia 35, 49, 112
Irazú Volcano 56, 58
Isla Damas 84
Isla del Caño 89
Islas Catalinas 34
Jacó 118
Jardín Botánico Lankester 58
Jardín de Mariposas (Monteverde) 67
La Flor Finca Agroecológica La Flor 22
La Fortuna 70
Lago de Coter 37

Laguna de Arenal 37, 70
La Pavona 97, 105
Liberia 37, 72, 112
Liberia Airport 63
Manuel Antonio 85
Manzanillo 102
Mistico Park 71
Moín 118
Monteverde 29, 66, 110
Monteverde Cloud Forest Biological Reserve 66
Montezuma 77
Museo de Arte y Diseño Contemporáneo (San José) 11, 46
Museo de Biología Marina (Heredia) 50
Museo de Cultura Popular (Heredia) 50
Museo de los Niños (San José) 47
Museo del Oro Precolombino (San José) 10, 44, 116
Museo Histórico Cultural Juan Santamaría (Alajuela) 11, 54
Museo Municipal de Cartago 57
Museo Nacional (San José) 46
Museo Nacional del Jade (San José) 45
Nicoya 74
Nosara 77
Papagayo Peninsula 74
Parque Central (Alajuela) 53
Parque Central (Heredia) 49
Parque Internacional La Amistad 73
Parque Marino del Pacífico (Puntarenas) 10, 12, 82
Parque Nacional Barra Honda 76
Parque Nacional Braulio Carrillo 51, 105, 118
Parque Nacional Cahuita 11, 98, 99
Parque Nacional Carara 83, 107
Parque Nacional Corcovado 37, 78, 79, 89, 117
Parque Nacional Manuel Antonio 10, 24, 37, 78, 85, 109
Parque Nacional Marino Ballena 86
Parque Nacional Palo Verde 76
Parque Nacional Rincón de la Vieja 37, 73
Parque Nacional San José 46
Parque Nacional Santa Rosa 36
Parque Nacional Tortuguero 13, 92, 96, 103, 117
Parque Zoológico Simón Bolívar (San José) 47
Península de Nicoya 36, 37, 72, 74
Península de Osa 79, 88, 114

Playa Cacao (Golfito) 90
Playa Cocles 100, 101
Playa Conchal 75
Playa el Chino 100, 101
Playa Escondida 85
Playa Grande 75
Playa Manzanillo 101, 102
Playa Montezuma 77
Playa Puerto Viejo 101
Playa Sámara 36, 77
Playa Tamarindo 36
Playa Ventanas 87
Poás Volcano 10, 13, 55, 61
Ponderosa Adventure Park 73
Potrero 37
Puerto Limón 96, 115, 118, 119
Puerto Viejo de Sarapiquí 52
Puerto Viejo de Talamanca 36, 99, 103
Puntarenas 37, 63, 78, 82, 115
Punta Uva 36
Quepos 11, 84, 91, 107
Refugio Nacional de Vida Silvestre Golfito 91
Reserva Biológica Bosque Nuboso Monteverde (Monteverde) 68
Reserva Bosque Nuboso Santa Elena (Monteverde) 66
Reserva Curi-Cancha 110
Reserva Playa Tortuga (Uvita) 87
Rey Curré 115
Ruinas De La Parroquia (Cartago) 56
Sámara 36, 77
San José 22, 24, 30, 40, 44, 97, 104, 107, 112, 114, 115, 118, 119
Santa Ana 44, 61
Santa Cruz 75
Santa Elena 66, 77, 109, 110, 111
Santa Teresa 37
Sarchí 32, 56
Spirogyra Butterfly Garden (San José) 12, 47
Tamarindo 37, 75
Tambor 37
Teatro Nacional (San José) 10, 45
Tortuguero 106
Tortuguero Parque Nacional Tortuguero 106
Turrialba 35, 59
Turrialba Volcano 59, 117
Turtle Beach (Parque Nacional Tortuguero) 97
Uvita 36, 85, 115
Valle Central 40
Valle del General 88
Valle Orosí 60
Yatama Ecolodge 52
Zarcero 56

WE WANT TO HEAR FROM YOU!

Did you have a great holiday? Is there something on your mind? Whatever it is, let us know! Whether you want to praise the guide, alert us to errors or give us a personal tip – MARCO POLO would be pleased to hear from you. Please contact us by email:

sales@heartwoodpublishing.co.uk

We do everything we can to provide the very latest information for your trip. Nevertheless, despite all of our authors' thorough research, errors can creep in. MARCO POLO does not accept any liability for this.

PICTURE CREDITS

Cover photo: Manuel Antonio National Park (AWL Images: M. Simoni)
Photos: V. Alsen (127); huber-images: P. Canali (78/79, 104/105, 109), P. Giocoso (22), R. Taylor (10, 54, 85, 89); Laif: Gonzalez (45, 49), A. Schumacher (110/111); mauritius images: M. Simoni (8/9), mauritius images/age fotostock: J. C. Muñoz (88); mauritius images/Alamy (11, 29 rechts, 36/37), S. Bay (13), S. bly (26/27), T. Cohen (90), K. Day (67), R. Duchaine (33), L. Fendt (115), S. Pearce (112/113), M. Santos (25), Sunshine Pics (75), M. Vilbas (103), C. Wise (76); mauritius images/Alamy/Autumn Sky Photography: L. Fendt (Klappe hinten); mauritius images/Alamy/MShieldsPhotos: H. Laub (32/33); mauritius images/Alamy/Persimmon Pictures.com (70); mauritius images/Alamy/robertharding (57); mauritius images/Alamy/Travelib prime (55); mauritius images/Alamy/Universal Images Group North America LLC (53); mauritius images/Danita Delimont: C. Miller Hopkins (2/3), M. Niles (62/63); mauritius images/Hemis.fr: R. Mattes (6/7); mauritius images/imageBROKER: H. Laub (14/15), Siepmann (98), K. Wothe (50); mauritius images/John Warburton-Lee: M. Simoni (40/41); mauritius images/Minden Pictures: S. Kennerknecht (96); mauritius images/Radius Images (28/29); mauritius images/robertharding (72/73), M. Simoni (60); H. Mielke (21, 58, 68, 92/93); Schapowalow: G. Cozzi (12), R. Schmid (Klappe vorne außen, Klappe vorne innen, 1); Schapowalow/SIME: P. Canali (16/17); shutterstock: butabanatravel (122/123), Creative Cat Studio (30), M. Dudarev (34/35), Inspired By maps (124/125), Lucas Kovarik (6/7), N. Naum (86), M. Rehak (100/101), Galina Savina (82)

3rd Edition – fully revised and updated 2024

Worldwide Distribution: Heartwood Publishing Ltd, Bath, United Kingdom
www.heartwoodpublishing.co.uk

Authors: Volker Alsen, Birgit Müller-Wöbcke
Editor: Franziska Kahl
Picture editor: Susanne Mack
Cartography: © MAIRDUMONT, Ostfildern (pp. 38–39, 106, 108, 110, outside jacket, pull-out map; © MAIRDUMONT, Ostfildern, using data from OpenStreetMap, licence CC-BY-SA 2.0 (pp. 42–43, 46, 64–65, 80–81, 94–95)
Cover design and pull-out map cover design: bilekjaeger_Kreativagentur with Zukunftswerkstatt, Stuttgart
Page design: Langenstein Communication GmbH, Ludwigsburg

Heartwood Publishing credits:
Translated from the German by Thomas Moser, Mo Croasdale
Editors: Rosamund Sales, Kate Michell
Prepress: Summerlane Books, Bath
Printed in India

MARCO POLO AUTHOR
VOLKER ALSEN

Volker has been living in Latin America for over three decades. He travels constantly and knows the region like no other. "I love the lush nature, the people in this part of the world and their way of life," he enthuses. Volker runs two small hotels in Costa Rica *(posadanena.com)*, and he uses his insider knowledge in his specialist agency Alautentico *(alautentico.com)* to help independent travellers experience the best trips possible.

DOS & DON'TS

HOW TO AVOID SLIP-UPS AND BLUNDERS

DON'T EAT SHARK FIN SOUP

Do you see *sopa de aleta de tiburón* on the menu? Don't order it – although the trade in shark fins has long been banned, it is still widespread on the Pacific coast.

DON'T BOOK TOO MANY EXPENSIVE ACTIVITIES

Costa Rica is sometimes more expensive than expected. It's worth comparing the costs of national park admission fees, for example, and planning well. Sure: whizzing over the treetops is a must, but some zip-lining operators charge more than those in Europe.

DON'T DRIVE AT NIGHT

Deep potholes are common on the roads, obstacles are unlit and sometimes the road ends nowhere: at night it's best to leave the car at home.

DON'T SMOKE IN THE WRONG PLACE

Costa Rica has strict non-smoking laws. Smoking is forbidden by law in all public facilities, hotels (on the entire premises), restaurants (even open-air ones), bars, buses, markets, and in parks and on beaches. Failure to observe the law could bring you a hefty fine!

DON'T UNDERESTIMATE THE CURRENTS

Be careful when swimming: there are dangerous currents all along the Pacific coast and on the southern Atlantic – sometimes even when the water only comes up to your knees. More than 100 people drown because of currents every year. There aren't many lifeguards on beaches. Never swim in the open sea, but keep to the bays. Never let small children out of your sight.